CW01466909

Living Life
in the
Last Lane

Chris Spicer

malcolm down
PUBLISHING

British Library Cataloguing in Publication Data
A catalogue record for this book is available from the British Library.
ISBN 978-1-917455-32-9

Design by Hannah Thompson
Printed in the UK

Dedication

This book is dedicated to the memory of our dear friend, Vince Ricketts, a man of God whose unshakeable faith, infectious smile, and insatiable appetite for God's Word – all demonstrated in a world of hurt – epitomised the reality of the apostle Paul's words, 'We do not lose heart. Though our outer self is wasting away, our inner self is being renewed day by day.'[1]

---

1.   2 Corinthians 4:16, ESV

Contents

Acknowledgements

Given that the author is in his late seventies, it comes as no surprise that the list of people who have knowingly or unknowingly inspired him to write this book is too extensive to include everyone. But, if you have in any way journeyed with him, he would want to acknowledge a debt of gratitude for your encouragement, inspiration and wisdom along the way.

That said, it would be remiss not to mention certain individuals who have made this publication possible. Firstly, thanks to his youngest daughter, Hannah Thompson for her work on the book cover; foundational input from author Mark Stibbe; editorial help from Sheila Jacobs; illustrations by Taffy Davies; foreword by Stuart Bell and a big shout out to Malcolm Down and his team for taking this book through the publishing process. Last, but by no means least a heartfelt thanks must go out to his wife, Tina – for without her love, patience and companionship *Living Life in the Last Lane* would not be possible.

Foreword

It's a real honour to write the foreword for *Living Life in the Last Lane*. Chris Spicer has penned a timely and deeply relevant book – one that speaks not only to the changing seasons of life, but also to the opportunities that lie ahead for those willing to embrace transition with faith and courage.

This book has landed at a particularly meaningful moment for me personally, and for our wider family. Many of the themes Chris explores have echoed loudly in our own journey over the past few years. After more than four decades in ministry, I now find myself in a significant period of transition.

I've had the privilege of founding a national network of churches called Ground Level, and for many years, I served as the senior pastor of Alive Church – a vibrant, multi-site church based in the heart of Lincoln. Two years ago, I handed over the leadership of Ground Level, and more recently, I released the local church into the capable hands of a new leadership team.

Although my wife, Irene, often jokes that I've been talking about transition since I was thirty years old, it's been remarkable how many people now ask me what it feels like to be retired. While we've been very intentional about passing on leadership, both Irene and I firmly believe that we still have productive and valuable years ahead – years that we pray will continue to bear fruit for the kingdom.

In many cultures, the process of ageing is understood very differently. In some nations, age and experience are not sidelined but seen as essential qualifications for leadership and wisdom. Chris does an excellent job of inviting us to rethink what later life can – and should – look like in God's economy.

Whether you're navigating your own transition, supporting someone else in theirs, or simply curious about how to make your years count in every season, this book will challenge, inspire and encourage you. Chris brings wisdom, humour and insight to a conversation that the Church desperately needs to have.

My hope is that *Living Life in the Last Lane* will serve as both a mirror and a map: reflecting where you are and helping you discern where God might be leading you next.

Enjoy the journey.

Stuart Bell, BEM
Founding pastor of Alive Church and founding leader of
the Ground Level Network

An Open Letter
to Readers

Dear Reader,

For those wondering why a septuagenarian author would make an effort to write about *Living Life in the Last Lane*, the author would like to make it clear that this book is born out of a conviction that:

- Living through a so-called *Longevity Revolution* will demand a major rethink concerning our attitude to an ageing population;

- In God's economy old age was never intended to be an over-the-hill experience. Although our physical being might be in decline, our inner self can still aspire to new levels of spiritual revelation;

- There is a vacant seat that seniors should occupy so as to *cheer* and *steer* this present generation;

- Seniors need to be challenged to come off the sidelines and zealously give their absolute best;

- Leaders ignore the experience, expertise, wisdom, knowledge and networking ability of an older generation at their peril;

- Christianity needs a biblical rather than a secular view of age and the ageing process;

- We need to build *inter-generational communities* in which all ages serve, worship, listen to and learn from each other;

- It's time for seniors to embrace the role of 'elders in the gate' and share their wisdom with the next generation.

May the Holy Spirit journey with you as you read, so that together we may change our culture and build communities that truly reflect the heart of a inter-generational heavenly Father.

Chris Spicer

NOTE: Throughout this publication terms like elders, senior citizens, seniors, third agers and retirees are used to describe an ageing population. None are meant to be in any way condescending, belittling or offensive, they are just different ways to describe age and the ageing process.

1

Hidden Assets

On a winter's morning in 1848, an American carpenter made an incredible discovery that would ultimately revolutionise the West Coast of North America. In partnership with a German immigrant, James Marshall was overseeing the construction of a new timber sawmill. Situated on the 'American River' at a place known to the Indigenous Americans as 'Beautiful Valley' both men believed this to be the perfect location for their new logging venture. Little did they know that on this particular day, logging would be the last thing on their minds.

Today a simple monument marks the spot where more than 176 years earlier, a middle-aged builder from New Jersey spotted a few flakes of metal glistening in the morning sun. With thoughts of what he may or may not have discovered, even Marshall's weather-beaten face managed to break out in an uncharacteristic smile.

Once their find was verified, the partners tried their best to keep things under wraps. But good news travels fast. In a matter of weeks, newspapers all over America were reporting about gold being discovered at

Sutter's Mill in California, comments enough to spark a worldwide stampede.

What followed was the greatest mass migration of people in the history of the Western Hemisphere. While most were Americans, 300,000 men, women and children from Latin America, Europe, Australia and China descended on the fledgling state of California. Spending their life savings panning for gold, would-be prospectors inadvertently kickstarted the economy of the 'Golden State'. While suffering untold hardships in a lawless environment, these hardy individuals risked everything in the pursuit of this precious metal. Although, only lasting seven years, the Californian Gold Rush of 1848 to 1855 was one of the most significant events in shaping the West Coast of North America.

Mines to motherboards

Today gold still occupies a prominent place in the human psyche. From Olympic medals to wedding rings, gold symbolises longevity, success, value, power and beauty. From industry to dentistry, this highly prized product is sought after by individuals, corporations and nations alike.

In South Wales, England, the British Royal Mint have recently constructed a unique facility. Being the first of its kind in the world it's hoped the factory will annually extract gold from 4,000 tons of e-waste. As a highly efficient conductor, gold has become an integral part of electrical appliances. Calculators, laptops, televisions and iPhones all contain a miniscule measure of pure gold. By recovering precious metal from e-waste, the Royal Mint is hoping to cash in on a twenty-first century gold rush. While athletes race for it, individuals collect it and nations build their economy on it, gold is a highly valued commodity that no one can afford to ignore.

But what if the intrinsic value of this precious metal and humanity's quest for it was an allegory, a metaphor regarding the undiscovered wisdom, expertise, knowledge and experience found in an older generation? What if this was a narrative about organisational leaders becoming more innovative in extracting gold from the old? What if churches, companies and communities alike took a fresh look at an ageing population? What if this was an invitation to adventure with God and discover untold wealth in what others tend to treat as generational waste?

Although requiring a paradigm shift of gargantuan proportions, imagine a world in which:

- Organisational leaders saw the elderly as a fundamental part in the affairs of heaven on earth;

- Society believed that older people were a blessing to embrace, rather than a burden to ignore or humour;

- Entrepreneurial leaders devised new ways of extracting the wisdom, experience and expertise resident in an older generation?

- And finally, imagine a world in which senior citizens not only became comfortable in their own skin, but given the opportunity found new

ways to leave a positive legacy, in and for the
next generation!

There's a new age waiting to be discovered, but only those
who think inter-generationally will find it. To ignore, isolate
and intern seniors in age-related ghettos should have
no part in the economy of heaven on earth. Old is gold,
and society needs to rethink its strategy. Ageism might
humorously or disparagingly speak of seniors as being 'over
the hill', but the reality is, there is gold in those hills. As
Nicky Gumbel, an Anglican priest, known as the developer
of the Alpha course, puts it:

I'm longing to see people who have been trapped
by ageism ordained. Research shows that the most
productive decade of your life is 60 to 70. The second
is 70 to 80. And the third is 50-60. The church has
not adapted to this. Caleb was still as strong at 85 as
he had been in his youth . . . We have a vision to find
6,000 Calebs, so every Church of England church has
a focal minister.[2]

As the world's population gets older, people are having
to rethink what living in the last lane really means. Older
people are now seeing that they have a key role in the
affairs of heaven on earth. This cultural and attitudinal shift
means that while some retirees may prefer to spend their

---

2. www.premierchristianity.com/interviews/alpas-nicky-gumbel-on-retiring-from-htb-
   evangelising-the-world-and-addressing-the-world-racism/13503.article (accessed
   14.7.25).

time relaxing at home pursuing their hobbies, others are looking for a more adventurous way of life.

Those who care win!

Scientists have recently discovered fossils of what they believe to be 'the world's first elderly human with clear signs of aging and impairment'.[3] Believing that he belonged to a nomadic tribe of hunter-gatherers, scientists suggest that the person in question was a 'disabled man who may have had trouble walking or carrying a heavy load'.[4] Taking all these factors into consideration the conclusion is that these are the remains of an elderly disabled man, who lived as long as he did because he was a valued member of his community who experienced a high level of social support.

Over the centuries, society's view of seniors has been something of a roller-coaster ride. During the European Dark Ages, the ageing process was considered to be a 'positive evil', while seventeenth and eighteenth-century painters were commended for portraying the elderly with beauty, wisdom, dignity and experience. Then again, the Industrial Revolution may have produced altruistic leaders who built poorhouses and workhouses for those without families or finance. But those places tended to be harsh institutional environments. While offering a place to work, eat and sleep, the empathic caring community all humans need was sadly lacking.

---

3. www.timesofindia.indiatimes.com/science/500000-yrs-on-f...of-worlds-first-disabled-man-found/articleshow/6739479.cms (accessed 5.9.24).
4. www.silverbellhomestead.com/the-history-of-elder-care (accessed 24.7.25).

Having lived on the African continent, my wife learned first-hand how care for the elderly was embedded into their culture. In his excellent book *What Are Old People For,* Dr William Thomas writes how a friend who grew up on the Ivory Coast describes how these caring communities mark every stage of life by a rite of passage:

> These rites of passage provide social identity and prepare the youth for responsibilities of adulthood. Before Africa was colonized by Europe, the initiation was one of the most prominent ways education was provided to the young.[5]

He goes on to speak of how twenty-something men and women would transition from childhood into adulthood, then:

> After a person has productively lived his or her life as an adult in the community, he or she is honoured by a second initiation ... into the Elder circle. This usually happens around the age of sixty-five. These Elders, now masters of the school life, have the responsibility of facilitating the transition from childhood to adulthood of new generations ... The idea of Elders as "library" also reveals the fact that only the Elders have full access to the tribe's knowledge base ... In this community the older you are the more respect you receive.[6]

5. William H. Thomas, *What Are Old People For?: How Elders Will Save the World* (St Louis, MO: VanderWyk & Burnham, 2007), p. 59.
6. Thomas, *What Are Old People For?*, p. 59.

In a world that values the vigour of youth above the wisdom of years, historians can point to a particular time when our appreciation for the elderly began to decline.

Human beings, out of necessity, had to search for food and grazing. Living on the edge of starvation, village living was replaced by a nomadic lifestyle. These travelling communities could ill-afford to slow down for the frail, sick and elderly. In the same way predators pick-off those too weak to keep up with a migrating herd, so those trailing behind a nomadic community became highly vulnerable.

The Jewish Torah speaks of the much-hated Amalekites as attacking 'all the stragglers at your rear [those] faint and weary'.[7] With the sick, weak and elderly lagging behind, the enemy developed a cowardly strategy. So much so that in Jewish imagery, the Amalekites serve as a metaphor for 'attacking the weak'.

Transitioning from village living to a nomadic lifestyle became a social tipping point, a moment in time that brought about a decline in elderly care; in the same way twenty-first century economic disbursement of the nuclear family is affecting the care and concern we presently have for an ageing population.

Houston we have a problem

In a world where ability is being sacrificed on the altar of ageism, humanity's angle of approach to age and the ageing process is thwart with challenges. Once seen as a blessing to embrace, rather than a burden to escape, society is

---

7.   See Deuteronomy 25:17-18, NASB.

facing an age-old problem. If such thinking was confined to governments, companies, social and health care that would be bad enough, but sadly ageism has found its way into religious institutions.

Much of Christianity's present methodology for handling the elderly is missing out on a vital part of God's mission. The ghetto mentality that segregates the elderly into age-related social groups is an old paradigm that is wasting a precious resource. An old wineskin that is cracked and liable to leak a most precious commodity. Such structures will in time prove incapable of containing God's end-time inter-generational plan. We stand at a societal tipping-point. And just as the flight crew of Apollo 13 found their crippled lunar module unsuitable for their mission, the present construct of Western churches, regarding an ageing population, has become a vehicle unfit for purpose. Surrounded by faulty generational connections, the present situation is a ticking timebomb that could either implode or explode at any moment. A perfect storm in which 'old rage' could become a reality.

For Christianity to find its way back, the Church will need to position itself on the cutting edge of a communal renaissance. A resurgence of community life, as God originally intended, initiated by leaders thinking inter-generational, rather than mono or multigenerational. To merely celebrate a congregation of mixed age groups is to fall short of the divine mandate. Our mission is to mirror the inter-generational heartbeat of a loving heavenly Father; to demonstrate the true essence of the Church as a nuclear family. An environment in which all ages, despite their cultural, social or fiscal background are seen to be doing life together. Perhaps then, society will sit up and take notice of a visible demonstration of God's kingdom manifesto.

To create a potential dream out of this present nightmare, leaders will need to eject a dysfunctional belief system. Thinking that views old age in terms of decline, dementia, disease, disability, dependence and death and no longer give preference to a youth-orientated programme that ignores an older generation; transitioning to a church construct that fuels the flickering embers of hope, still smouldering in those considered to be over the hill.

Turning the page on age

As news of the early Church spread throughout the Roman Empire, rumours began to circulate as to the beliefs and behaviour of those who had given up their pagan lifestyle to follow the teachings of Jesus. In their defence, a Church leader and writer by the name of Tertullian, who lived in the late second and early third centuries, wrote a brief explanation as to how Christian communities differed from their pagan neighbours.

But even the putting into practice of so great a love as this brands us with a mark of censure in the opinion of some. 'See,' say they, 'how they love each other!' ... and, 'how ready they are to die for each other![8]

That non-partisan love shown to Greek and Gentile, men and women, old and young alike, was in part what made the first-century Church uniquely different. In this they mirrored the words of the Old Testament prophets, who spoke of an environment in which 'young and old [celebrated] life together',[9] a time when 'Old men and old women will ... sit on benches on the streets and spin tales, move around safely with their canes – a good [place] to grow old in. And boys and girls will fill the public parks, laughing and playing – a good [place] to grow up in.'[10]

While modern society is working hard to combat *racism* and *sexism*, what of the age-old problem of *ageism*? When will we see a similar rejection of that awful, demonic stronghold? Voicing the words of the prophet Joel, Peter, on the Day of Pentecost spoke of the difference the coming of the Holy Spirit would make.[11] He would bring an end to *racism* by empowering 'all flesh'; creating an environment in which 'sons and daughters shall prophesy'. Here *sexism* would become obsolete and *ageism* banished as, 'young men shall see visions, and ... old men shall dream dreams' (ESV).

8. *Apologeticus*, 'Tertullian (c. 160-c. 225 AD) on Christian worship', www. deovivendiperchristum.wordpress.com, 11 August, 2013, (accessed 28.7.2025).
9. Jeremiah 31:13, paraphrased.
10. Zechariah 8:4, *MSG*.
11. Acts 2:17-21; Joel 2:28-32.

If first-century Christians looked in on the twenty-first century Church, they would probably find few comparisons. The more observant onlooker might ask, what happened to those inter-generational communities which the Holy Spirit initiated? And having mentally stripped away the paraphernalia of performance-centred gatherings, they might enquire as to what happened to the practice of doing life together? Looking for inter-generational answers, they might quiz church leaders as to how they plan to unearth the gold presently buried in the old.

When church leaders opt for a youth centric culture and throw the elderly under a proverbial bus called *Relevance*, a radical rethink into how we do church becomes crucial. In God's economy a person's final years are meant to be the *pinnacle* of all that has gone before. No one should be left feeling like a deserted mine or a discarded motherboard. In a society that perceives the ageing process as one of no possibility, seniors from every social, cultural and fiscal background will need to maintain high levels of expectation in the face of all opposing factors.

You played my crescendo

In his video teaching on *Leadership: The Art of Possibility*,[12] Ben Zander, who conducts the Boston Philharmonic Orchestra beautifully illustrates how living life in the last lane is intended to be. As a musical conductor, his position is one of great influence. Wielding his baton and striking

---

12. Video, *Leadership: An Art of Possibility* – Groh Productions, www.grohtv.com, 2013 (accessed 14.7.25).

a variety of dynamic poses, his photograph appears on the front cover of numerous orchestral recordings. The only musician not to make a sound, his power, though immense, depends on his ability to make others powerful. His role is to awaken possibility in every member of the orchestra. To create a beautiful symphonic sound to which an appreciative audience give a standing ovation.

Before rehearsals begin, Ben has a habit of placing a blank piece of paper on every musician's music stand. He does so with an invitation to write anything they believe will improve the orchestra's public performance. On one occasion a young lady wrote the words, 'You're not making enough crescendo'. The piece they were rehearsing was a Bruckner movement, a musical score that builds towards a loud and glorious finale. That evening, Ben Zander caused the orchestra to play a huge crescendo. Straight after, an overly excited young lady made her way to the conductor's podium. Struggling to contain her appreciation, when an opportune moment presented itself, she enthusiastically expressed her thanks saying, 'You did my crescendo!'

Life is a musical composition, created in such a way as to ultimately bring glory to God. Harmonising together, every season of life is intended to resonate with what the original composer had in mind. The four movements of Childhood, Adolescence, Adulthood and Old Age are intended to symphonise together in such a way as to produce one cohesive sound. Although the tempo may change, no section of this human masterpiece is meant to take the pre-eminence over the other. Each movement journeys the composition towards a glorious crescendo called Old Age. So, let's 'Stand up in the presence of the aged, show respect for the elderly and revere your God. I am the LORD.'[13]

For:

by lionizing youth and using the benchmarks of a healthy adulthood as the gold standard of wellbeing, contemporary society has created a simple but radical reinterpretation of age and ageing . . . Old age has been recast as a merciless descent from the apex of youth – a hurtling fall and a peculiar form.[14]

When looking back on life's symphony, those living life in the last lane want nothing more than to express thanks to those orchestral leaders conducting their final years and express their sincere thanks in saying, 'You played my crescendo.'

Ripe old age

Although the phrase 'ripe old age' is used to celebrate longevity, what if these words had a more organic interpretation? Rather than just applauding long life, these words represented a season of life, to which all others have been heading? Such thinking would alter our concept of the ageing process from a decline into decrepitude, to a season of fulfilment and fruition.

Growing old is difficult and often demanding. But if our *belief* affects our *behaviour* and ultimately what we *become* – then filling our minds with numerous age-related

13. Leviticus 19:32, NIV.
14. Thomas, *What Are Old People For?*, p. 84.

challenges, which may or may not happen, could have a direct bearing on how we handle our later years.

Whether we use the phrase 'ripe old age' humorously or disparagingly, its true meaning is more profound than most people think. Study any classic English dictionary and the word 'ripe' will often be spoken of in terms of:

- Completely developed

- Reaching its best state

- Fit for use

- Advancing to a place of maturity

- Fully qualified by continuous improvement

Using these definitions, those who have reached a 'ripe old age' have stepped into a season of life in which they have become prepared, perfected, fully qualified by previous improvements, so as to achieve their best state of life. Why, then, shouldn't this perfection in growth not refer to old age? A key moment in time in which older people are enjoying the fruition of all that has gone before. To quote Thomas again:

Imagine growing into an old age defined by full development, maturity, awareness, readiness and advancement; it would truly be an opportune time. Unfortunately, society has not followed the botanists' lead. We are mired in a highly negative view of ageing that envisions a one-way trip down the long road toward disease, dementia, disability, and death. Peaches may ripen, but human beings, it seems, cannot.[15]

All of life is spent ageing, yet to many, old age remains a season of no possibility. When this philosophy becomes paramount, the elderly are treated like buried gold with their true value hidden. The symphony of life builds towards a decrescendo and while plants grow towards a point in which they flourish and bloom, the same cannot be said of human beings. This one-sided narrative has to change. Humanity needs to turn the page on age, because living life in the last lane has far more to offer than society would have us believe.

Ageing has its advantages

Although growing old can be difficult and demanding, some reckon that the ageing process has benefits. Believing the second half of life transcends the first, those who think this way would advocate that in areas like Self, Society and Space, ageing has its advantages.

- **Self** – While leaving a full-time career and experiencing a change in social roles can result in a decline in self-esteem, generally speaking older adults tend to be less self-conscious. Understanding that the universe no longer revolves around them, the self-absorbed me, mine and more mindset becomes less dominate with age. Although freedom

---

15. Thomas, *What Are Old People For?*, p. 13.

from former inhabitations can sometimes prove negative – such as inappropriate comments and behaviour – the elderly tend to be less concerned with self-perception. In terms of selfhood, the older we get, the more honest we become. Accepting our physical and cognitive limitations, seniors take on a more positive perception of selfhood. Less self-absorbed, their source of pride is less self-focused. Adopting a more altruistic lifestyle, an ageing generation become ideal candidates for volunteerism – a truth sadly lost on many organisational leaders.

- **Society** – The research also reckons that older people tend to become more selective in their relationships. With little time for shallow, meaningless connections, solitude can be celebrated rather than avoided. Not needing to follow the crowd to find their identity, older people are more self-assured and less possessions-orientated. Black and white issues become less certain and they no longer need others to grant them permission to be true to themselves. Something the Scottish poet Jenny Joseph vocalised in her poem, 'WARNING: When I am an old woman I shall wear purple'.[16]

  Although becoming less self-conscious than their younger self, older people can also become hyper-sensitive as to their role in society and how others perceive it.

---

16. www.scottishpoetrylibrary.org.uk (accessed 24.7.25).

- **Space** – As people age, the past, present and future all seem to collide into one cosmic timeframe. A fresh interest in ancestry and a revised awareness of their surroundings is somewhat characteristic of old age. For many, death becomes less feared, and although their younger self avoided it, an interest in eternity becomes more prevalent. This is a reality that organisations like Faith in Later Life (www.faithinlaterlife.org) and Silver Cord ministries (www.silvercord.co.uk)[17] have based their whole charitable enterprise on.

By rehearsing the advantages of old age, we quieten the voices that incessantly speak of the disadvantages. For modern society persists in portraying old people as a physical representation of a vintage vehicle. Lacking the speed and agility of their modern counterparts, they are seen as expensive items to keep. In constant need of care and attention, they're liable at any given moment to break down and die on us. Framed around a declinist mentality, the common view of old age is one of decline into decrepitude. Disadvantages that tend to tip the balance in favour of a youth-centric society.

Comfortable in their own skin

If society is to change its attitude towards age and the ageing process, it will need pathfinders to exemplify a different way

17. www.faithinlaterlife.org; www.silvercord.co.uk (accessed 28.7.25).

of living life in the last lane. Everyone handles the passage of time differently, from quiet resignation to outlandish behaviour. Some individuals will go to extraordinary lengths to stop the inevitable onset of old age.

Scanning the mirror daily in search of those tell-tale signs of ageing does little to help our mental well-being. While snakes shed their wrinkled skin and birds exchange their worn-out feathers, mammals keep the skin they were born with. Pandering to this age-old problem, some dermatologists are now advocating that 'wrinkled, sagging skin is not the inevitable result of growing older. It is a disease you can fight'.[18] Those who prescribe to this kind of warped ideology should realise that by our mid-twenties our skin begins to lose its elasticity.

To look enviously at the young and wish we could amalgamate their youthful looks and energy with our expertise and experience is pointless. There is a divine reason for every season, a God-given moment in time for which we are called to celebrate not commiserate. So maybe the answer to this age-old problem is to wear our wrinkles with honour and become comfortable in our own skin. To echo those New Testament sentiments that say 'we're not giving up. How could we! Even though on the outside it often looks like things are falling apart on us, on the inside, where God is making new life, not a day goes by without his unfolding grace'.[19]

When it comes to the ageing process, we are a society of extremes. At one end of the spectrum are those evergreen veterans who are adept at reinventing themselves to

---

18. https://time.com/archive/6667444/health-skin-deep/ (accessed 24.7.25).
19. 2 Corinthians 4:16, *MSG*.

suit the changing seasons. At the other extreme there are those who dress, speak and act like dishevelled has-beens. Growing old gracefully requires God's grace. While practising a balance diet, exercise, sleep and social interaction is important, for those following the teachings and life of Jesus Christ, spiritual disciplines like prayer, Bible reading and Holy Communion are essential. For although we live in a profoundly ageist society where youth is venerated and old age is vilified, the world needs pathfinders who will celebrate God's love no matter the age or stage of life.

No society can afford to ignore those hidden assets found in the elderly. Any secular or spiritual governmental system that refuses to care for and resource the wisdom, knowledge, experience and expertise found in an ageing population will fail to reach its full potential. If the Second World War teaches us anything, it is that when a nation faces a crisis, leaders need to re-evaluate and re-engage its senior citizens.

To reach a 'ripe old age' is more than applauding longevity, it's enjoying a season of fruitfulness and fulfilment. All of which sets the scene for a grand finale, a moment in time in which the heavenly conductor will complete and complement our life with a glorious crescendo.

Question marks!

- Who or what is presently excavating the gold of expertise, experience, wisdom and networking ability in your life?

- Every season of life has its reason. What is your passion and purpose for this stage of your life?

- If you could choose life's crescendo, what would it look and sound like?

- God's mandate for maturity is to reach a 'ripe old age', a season of fulfilment and fruitfulness. Is that your experience? If not, is there anything you could change?

2

The Third Act

For those of a certain age and disposition, the television sitcom *Dad's Army*[20] will forever be a popular source of personal entertainment. Taking fourth place in the 2004 BBC poll to find Britain's Best Sitcom, this much-loved TV show has, over the years, become a firm family favourite. Outlining the struggles of a Second World War local Home Guard platoon, great acting alongside unforgettable script-writing has created situational comedy at its best.

Situated in fictional Walmington-on-Sea on the south coast of England, this imaginary location became ground-zero for a possible Nazi invasion. Intended to combat a superior fighting force, this volunteer army was nothing more than a group of male misfits. Their group dynamic consisted of a pessimistic Scottish undertaker; a black-marketer; a home-bird bank clerk; an elderly orderly; an old warhorse and local butcher – all led by a self-appointed, pompous local bank manager. Yet this mismatch of dubious individuals proved to be an act of sheer genius. Collectively this band of brothers managed to show how old age,

---

20.   TV sitcom, BBC One, 1968-1977.

incompetence and arrogance was a greater threat to the British Isles than any invading force.

With catchphrases like, 'We're doomed', 'Don't panic', 'You stupid boy,' and 'Don't tell him, Pike', the series has influenced British popular culture by becoming an integral part of English humour.

In true British style we might laugh at the antics of this motley crew, but the reality on which this series is based was no laughing matter.

In May 1940, England was on the brink of an imminent Nazi invasion. Having quickly overrun the rest of Europe, the infamous Third Reich had the British Isles in its sights. The thought of German jackboots marching up Whitehall and the Nazi swastika flying over Buckingham Palace galvanised the nation to delay the inevitable. Those unable to join the regular army because of their age were asked to join a people's army. Later called the Home Guard, what this rag-tag militia lacked in firepower, it made up for with passion and determination. Unarmed and lacking uniforms, this volunteer army became Britain's frontline of defence. As a battle-ready body of elderly men, they earned the nickname 'Dad's Army'.

It's no laughing matter

It would be fair to say that people in the West exhibit a strange ambivalence when it comes to all things old. We tend to revere old *objects*; we restore vintage vehicles, collect antique jewellery, and enjoy a well-aged wine. And yet we also fail to revere old *people*. When someone prefaces any reference to a person with the words *age* and *old*, the tone is often disparaging. They imply the person is unproductive and even worthless. This lack of honour is something urgently in need of correction. Western society needs a complete paradigm shift in what it believes about the elderly. We need to learn to regard those in their autumn years as a priceless resource rather than a disposable community.

Those who consider an ageing population as a social drain rather than a public asset should remember that in the United Kingdom, old people contribute an estimated £61 billion to the annual economy.[21] They also add social, technical, spiritual and emotional wealth to the fabric of society.

A sure way to destroy any group of people is either to accuse or make fun of them

The way we talk about the elderly reveals a lot about our attitudes. Some of the phrases that we often come up with in casual conversations betray our true feelings. We refer to *crotchety old ladies*, *grumpy old men* and *batty old biddies*. These idioms reveal the extent to which we unconsciously shame rather than honour our elderly population. If Western society is becoming more conscious of its historic racism (post George Floyd) and sexism (post Harvey Weinstein), the same cannot be said of our unconfessed ageism. Careless talk like this is a feature of many Western societies. In this, we lag far behind other parts of the world.

---

21. www.theguardian.com/society/2015/mar/24/better-society-for-older-people-live-discussion (accessed 14.7.25).

Take South Korea, for example, and indeed Korea generally. Like their Japanese and Chinese counterparts, the Koreans accept and respect their elders as a vital and vibrant part of society. They are not alone in this. Mediterranean and Latin cultures value the building of intergenerational communities. As we see in the hit movie *My Big Fat Greek Wedding* (2002), older people help care for the young while the breadwinners work outside the home.

This is not something we see in the West. In the UK, old people cease to have any use once they retire. This scorn derives from a Protestant work ethic that ties a person's value to their work. Older people are judged by what they can or cannot perform in terms of a professional skill.[22] An alien visiting from outer space would notice this within minutes. They would quickly detect the attitudes of young people towards the elderly – derision concerning their slow pace; irritation at the way old people occupy space on pavements or in supermarket aisles; anger towards them for driving slowly. When it comes to elderly people, society perceives them as a trial rather than as treasure. Sometimes, of course, seniors can be challenging. They can repeat the same stories over and over, display cranky attitudes, utter inappropriate comments and exhibit embarrassing habits. Old people can be eccentric, fussy and hard to please. But they are not rubbish that needs to be discarded; they are a resource that needs to be valued.

Historically, of course, we have not always disrespected the elderly. The values of the West were originally rooted and grounded in the Judaeo-Christian tradition – a tradition

---

22. Dr Bill Thomas, 'Old Age in Ancient Rome', www.changingAging.org (accessed 14.7.25).

based on the Bible. What the Bible teaches about the elderly is far removed from our current disrespect and disdain. Throughout the Hebrew and Christian Scriptures, readers are instructed to revere the elderly. In fact, God's Word to every generation is for the wise to seek the expertise of older people, just as King Solomon did. The wise are to seek the advice of older people, as a young pharaoh did with the ageing Joseph.[23] In the Bible 'old is good'.[24] Maybe the current negativity towards old age and old people is not just a sign of our lack of emotional, spiritual and moral health. Maybe it is also a sign of what happens when a society becomes less scriptural and more secular.[25]

Ready or not here I come!

While making fun of the elderly may be good for TV ratings, the long-term effect does little to correct what is paradoxically an age-old problem. Take the BBC, for example. Over the years it has managed to create numerous male curmudgeons and cantankerous old ladies. Leading the former is Victor Meldrew from the sitcom *One Foot in the Grave*. Played by Richard Wilson, Victor is a grumpy old man who is constantly complaining. Whether it's about children, cars, animals, power cuts, or neighbours, Victor often utters his trademark saying, 'I don't believe it' voted the top catchphrase by the viewing public. It's a phrase that 'expresses a mix of exasperation, world-weary resignation

---

23. 1 Kings 12:6; Genesis 45:8 – compare with Psalm 71:18.
24. Luke 5:39, ESV.
25. Ronald D. Witherup, *What Does the Bible Say About Old Age?* (New York: New City Press, 2019).

and fatalistic humour that will be familiar from many people's personal experience'.[26]

Leading the cantankerous old ladies is the self-opinionated, social climber Hyacinth Bucket, played by Patricia Routledge. Hyacinth insists that her surname should be pronounced "Bouquet". Performing in another hit BBC sitcom, *Keeping Up Appearances*, Hyacinth is the archetype of the older lady who has snobbery in buckets – or should that be bouquets? She is the kind of person you dread having as a neighbour or family member. Yet somewhere on your street or in your wider family there will be a Victor Meldrew or a Hyacinth Bucket. That's why we laugh when we watch these programmes. Even though they may be extreme irritations, we recognise these characters from people we know in real life. We enjoy Victor Meldrew and Hyacinth Bucket so much because we recognise aspects of them in others, or even in ourselves.

Yes, we laugh, but sooner or later we too will grow old. For those wanting to deny, delay, or disguise it, a multi-billion-dollar cosmetic industry awaits their custom. But masking its effects cannot halt the physical, emotional and spiritual onset of old age. Old age says to every one of us, 'Ready or not, here I come!' It's best to accept it and be prepared for it. We start to get old from the moment we are born. This is simply a fact of life. Nothing is to be gained by avoiding it. Everything is to be gained by embracing it. By adjusting our attitude, we can step gracefully into our senior years rather than descend into despondency. That

26. 'I don't believe it' – Victor Meldrew's catchphrase voted the nation's favourite, by Amardeep Bassey 11 October 2019, www.gloucestershirelive.co.uk (accessed 5.3.22).

said, it's not always easy to be positive about old age. One of the songs I grew up with in the Swinging Sixties was 'When I'm Sixty-Four'. Composed by Paul McCartney, this describes an imaginary conversation between a young man and his beloved. In it he asks whether she will still love him when he is getting old. Paradoxically, McCartney started writing it when he was only fourteen. The lyrics speak of a cynical anticipation of life in the last lane. While it shows McCartney's grasp of the physical, social, financial and relational complexities of ageing, it also taps into the negativity that characterises Western society's view of old age. Now in his early eighties, McCartney seemingly finds the song too juvenile to grapple with the crux of ageing, saying that 'If I were to write it now, I'd probably call it "When I'm 94".'[27]

'When I'm Sixty-Four' uncomfortably points out there are many physical challenges that accompany the ageing process. These begin earlier than we realise. From our mid-twenties, our bones lose calcium and become more brittle. Our skin loses its elasticity and age spots begin to appear. We start losing brains cells at a phenomenal rate. All the while, our weight begins to shift south. Our hair stops growing where we want it to and begins to grow in places no hair has grown before.

Then there's the way other people see us – especially younger people. In a revealing survey,[28] 2000 British young people (i.e. under the age of thirty) were asked to list tell-tale signs which in their opinion classified someone as being

27. https://faroutmagazine.co.uk/the-beatles-song-paul-mccartney-regrets-writing/ (accessed 14.7.25).
28. www.dailymail.co.uk/femail/aticle-9521811/The-tell-tale-signs-youre-getting-oldordering-cappuccino-Facebook.html (accessed 14.7.25).

old. They concluded that only old people would order a Cappuccino, ask for milk and two sugars in their tea, use Facebook, have a DVD collection, buy their underwear from Marks & Spencer, commonly use the thumbs-up emoji, groan when they sit down or stand up, and struggle to work the TV remote. Such people are officially 'past it'. Although age is relative, the same article also stated that no one over the age of fifty-one should wear jeans and no one over the age of forty-one should be seen on a scooter!

While our brain might still function as a twenty-something, our bodies will keep telling us otherwise. Sooner or later the ageing process will affect all of us. As it says in Ecclesiastes 12 (*MSG* version):

> In old age, your body no longer serves you so well. Muscles slacken, grip weakens, joints stiffen. The shades are pulled down on the world. You can't come and go at will. Things grind to a halt. The hum of the household fades away. You are wakened now by bird-song. Hikes to the mountains are a thing of the past. Even a stroll down the road has its terrors. Your hair turns apple-blossom white, Adorning a fragile and impotent matchstick body.[29]

Maybe you've seen *The Curious Case of Benjamin Button* (2009). In this hit movie, Brad Pitt plays a man who ages in reverse. Born old, he grows younger. This is, of course, a pipedream. Even if we work out in the gym every day and apply the finest anti-ageing cream every night, we are still

---

29. Ecclesiastes 12, *MSG*.

going to grow old. Ready or not, the ageing process is going to come to us all. And the last time I checked, the death rate for humans still stands at an unwavering 100 per cent.

Where can we find help in changing our beliefs and attitudes? The answer is in a book that has turned out to be ageless and unageing. In the Bible, we are encouraged to face the fact that our physical being is growing old and fading away.[30] But we are also exhorted to understand that with God's help, the spiritual part of our being can be constantly rejuvenated. As the apostle Paul put it, 'We do not lose heart. Though our outer self is wasting away, our inner self is being renewed day by day.'[31] It is the inner self that matters most because God has set eternity in our hearts.[32] We begin to grow young again when we live our immediate in the light of God's ultimate. Such a perspective allows us to prioritise who we are over what we do. Our value is not in our physical beauty or performance but in our attitudes and values. While *age* is a consequence of being human, our *attitude* to it is a personal choice

Wig adjustment

Returning from honeymoon to pastor a fledgling church, my wife, Tina, and I quickly found ourselves struggling through the uncharted waters of marriage and ministry. We needed help, and we needed it badly. In this season, that help came in the form of a senior saint by the name of Mrs Smith.[33]

30. 2 Corinthians 4:16, ESV
31. 2 Corinthians 4:16, ESV.
32. Ecclesiastes 3:11.
33. Name changed.

Originating from the East End of London, Mrs Smith now lived in a local old people's home.

A little context may help at this point.

Our church was situated in a small Northamptonshire market town that had experienced a population explosion. Originally a small quaint English village, the town was now made up of vast housing estates that surrounded it. While this looked like a good solution to the problem of overcrowding, it caused numerous social problems. The new town was nicknamed 'Dodge City'; and new residents wouldn't think twice about leaving under the cloak of darkness without paying their bills.

The ninety-year-old Mrs Smith was one of the most senior members of our congregation. With no friends or family nearby, her son – who lived some distance away – had asked us to look out for his ageing mother, something we were happy to do. Each Sunday morning, we would offer a lift to people without personal transportation. This included Mrs Smith. In her case, a door-to-door service was our only option. We therefore purchased a church minibus.

Perhaps 'minibus' is somewhat grandiose. The vehicle in question was a decommissioned National Health Service ambulance. Sadly, the 'blues and two's' (its siren and flashing lights) had been disabled. The spectacle of an ambulance racing through the town with its siren screaming, its lights flashing, and a sign that read, 'Calvary Pentecostal Church' (with the strapline, "We're here to save you") was very appealing! However, common sense prevailed.

Arriving at the old people's home every Sunday morning was always a venture into the unknown. Mrs Smith's unique dress code – characterised by a lack of colour coordination and extraordinary headgear – was the first thing we would encounter. In addition to her wardrobe malfunctions, the advancing years had not been kind. Suffering from major hair loss, she had been encouraged to wear a wig. Hairpieces back in the 70s were not what they are today. While the quality of the wig was questionable, the main issue was the fact that her central parting was all too often heading in the wrong direction. The dilemma I faced was twofold. Should I ignore the ill-placed offending item and put it all down to her eccentricity? That, for a self-confessed perfectionist, was always going to be difficult. Or should I attempt to help Mrs Smith preserve her dignity? In the end, Mrs Smith – who for some reason always called us George and Sonya – trusted us enough to allow us to make the necessary adjustments to her ill-fitting wig. *Pastoral Wig Adjustment* was not part of the curriculum in the Bible college I attended.

Yet what Mrs Smith lacked physically she made up for spiritually. To us she was the embodiment of the apostle Paul's words, 'Though our outer self is wasting away, our inner self is being renewed day by day.'[34] Although her outer shell was exhibiting the effects of the ageing process, her inner self was being spiritually renewed every day. In fact, she had more fire in her bones than Christians half her age. Her hopes and aspirations would regularly ignite a flame in others. Young people would make the effort to spend time in her presence.

Mrs Smith is a reminder that age is not just a number, it's a mindset. Our beliefs about old age affect our behaviour

---

34.   2 Corinthians 4:16, ESV.

as older people, and this in turn affects what we eventually become. While some people age gracefully, others do not. This can cause the young to dishonour old age.

The third act

Over the last 300 years there have been significant revolutions – American, French and Industrial to name just three. One of the most significant in our times is the so-called *Longevity Revolution*. Baby Boomers, those born between 1946 and 1964, are now living three decades longer than their great-grandparents. People are living to much greater ages. That being the case, how are we to change attitudes about the last phase of our lives? One answer is to go back to the ancient view of stories – a view that sees stories as made up of three acts (a beginning, a middle, and an end).

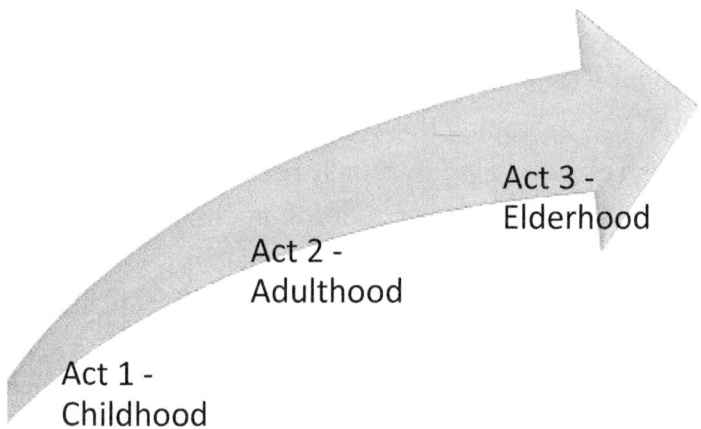

Act 3 -
Elderhood

Act 2 -
Adulthood

Act 1 -
Childhood

In a Ted Talk entitled 'Life's Third Act',[35] Jane Fonda talks about an old paradigm when it comes to understanding old age. She says that this is shaped like an arch (some would say like a hill). You're born, you peak in midlife, and then you decline into decrepitude. She argues that this is an outdated way of looking at our lives. Instead of two phases (ascent and descent), she contends that 'many people today – philosophers, artists, doctors, scientists – are taking a new look at what I call 'the third act' – the last three decades of life'. Instead of seeing life as two phases – going up a hill, and then being over the hill – she says we need a cultural revolution in which we see life as a three-act story. The third act – old age – is a season of perhaps the greatest possibility and the greatest productivity. Indeed, Act 3 is 'a developmental stage of life with its own significance, as different from midlife as adolescence is from childhood'.[36]

Jane Fonda makes a good point. Although Act 3 of our lives has its challenges – physical, medical, social, financial – society has downplayed the potential for living and giving in this final phase of our story. It has seen life as a two-staged process. It has relegated old people to those heading downhill, rather than as potential heroes entering the third act of their lives. It has characterised old age as the age of entropy – of wasting away, both physically and mentally.

It's time to change our beliefs about old age and leaders now need to rethink their strategy relating to those in Act 3 of their lives.

While it is possible to overstate the benefits of growing old, we should listen carefully to what Jane Fonda and

35. https://youtu.be/IHyR7p6_hn0?feature=shared,
36. Jane Fonda, 'Life's Third Act at TEDx Women', filmed December 2011.

many others are saying. The third act of life should not be seen as a decline into decrepitude but rather a vital part of our journey up a *spiral staircase*. While our 'outer self' finds stairs hard to climb, our 'inner self' can be continually ascending to higher levels of spiritual insight and intimacy.

As one Bible version puts it, 'our outward man is wearing out' while "the inward man is renewed day by day'.[37] This daily renewal becomes a progressive development of our spiritual being. Rather than accepting the ageing process as a downward spiral of no possibility, we perceive it to be an upward journey in which increased wisdom, understanding, balance and compassion encircles us. Our senior years are calling us to keep climbing, to look back and ahead so as to gain fresh spiritual insight that constantly renews our passion for the purpose of God.

37.   2 Corinthians 4:16, Jubilee Bible 2000.

Selinger is a retired lawyer who, at the age of fifty-seven, was diagnosed with ALS, more commonly known as Lou Gehrig's disease. Although this awful illness weakens the body, the mind remains intact. Having a love for reading and writing books, Neil joined a writer's group. During this phase, his body was wasting away. In an article for *The New York Times*, Peter Applebome told how Neil deteriorated 'with heart-breaking speed from cane to walker to wheelchair, to puréed food, an inability to speak and almost total immobility'. Yet, at the same time, something creative was happening on the inside. Neil wrote, 'As my muscles weakened, my writing became stronger.' He said, 'As I slowly lost my speech, I gained my voice. As I diminished, I grew. As I lost so much, I finally started to find myself.'[38] Rather than seeing his life as a downward spiral of no possibility, Neil saw himself ascending life's spiral staircase, an internal process which resulted in him feeling renewed daily. Instead of being 'on the way out', he was 'on the way up'. Although Neil was in no way old, he exemplified how we should face the physical challenges – as an opportunity for our inner self to ascend to 'the heavenly realms in Christ Jesus'.[39]

Room to let

All this is to say, Act 3 offers an extraordinary opportunity for expansion in inner creativity and vitality. In her book *Composing a Further Life: The Age of Active Wisdom*, social anthropologist Mary Catherine Bateson says, 'We have not

38. Peter Appleborne, 'Loss of Speech Evokes the Voice of a Writer', www.nytimes.com/2011/03/07nyregion/07towns.html (accessed 8.7.22).
39. Ephesians 2:6, NIV.

added decades to life expectancy by simply extending old age; instead, we have opened up a new space.'[40] She likens this to adding a new room to our home. As anyone who has built an extension will know, a new room alters every other aspect of a house.[41] The increase in life expectancy is therefore significant. Whether it's with work, marriage, parenting, finances, education, travel, fitness, identity, or belonging, we will all have an opportunity to fill this new room. Although the additional space may seem strange, seniors will need to learn how to occupy it.

One thing we should not do is treat this new extension as a waiting room – a space where we await the inevitable. Nor is this a space where we fritter away our lives with superficial and frivolous interests. When Jesus told the parable of the talents, the master encouraged his servants to 'Occupy till I come'.[42] This master was not telling them to occupy a space; he was telling them to use their time wisely. He was advocating that whatever life deals us, we should be about the Father's business. That is the key to occupying this extra room or making the most of our third act. It is living life in a way that will ultimately bring glory to God.

Refusing to slow down, some so-called retirees are searching for more adventurous ways to bring closure to their lives. 'Gone are the days of seniors relegated to sitting on porches swinging life away. Instead, they're out rock climbing, skydiving, and surfing. A growing movement of older adults refuse to let age define them or their lifestyle.'[43]

---

40. Mary Catherine Bateson, *Composing a Further Life* (New York: Knopf, 2020), p. 12.
41. Fonda, *Prime Time*, pp. ix-x
42. Luke 19:13, KJV.
43. https://nationallegal.com/80-is-the-new-60/#:~:text=Seniors%20are%20increasingly%20taking%20part,climbing%2C%20skydiving%2C%20and%20surfing (accessed 14.7.25).

Carl G. Jung was one of few psychologists who believed that the autumn of life was a season of growth and fulfilment, he once wrote, 'A human being would certainly not grow to seventy or eighty years old if this longevity had no meaning for the species to which he belongs. The afternoon of human life must also have a significance of its own, and cannot be merely a pitiful appendage to life's morning.'[44] Some researchers actually advocate that the most productive and influential season of human life is between the age of sixty and seventy.

Let's look at some examples of famous influencers.

Peter Roget invented the Thesaurus at the age of seventy-three.

Colonel Sanders started KFC at sixty-five.

Noah Webster completed his American Dictionary of the English Language at seventy.

Momofuku Ando invented Pot Noodles (for which many college students will be eternally grateful) at sixty-one.

Julie Child began her television cooking school at fifty-one.

Nelson Mandela was seventy-five when elected President of South Africa.

While society continues to classify the elderly as 'past it', it will miss out on valuable reinforcements within its ranks. A volunteer army is waiting to be enlisted by insightful leaders. While leaders think of old people as over the hill,

---

44. Carl G. Jung, *Modern Man in Search of a Soul* (New York: Harcourt, Brace and Co., 1933), p. 109.

they will miss out on the experience, expertise, knowledge and networking ability of seniors within their sphere.

It is time to root out and renounce such ageist attitudes. Those living in their autumn years should not be considered as fallen leaves to be swept aside and treated as compost for a youth-centric culture. We should never relegate grandparents to the corner of the room and tell them to sit silently, speaking only when spoken to. We should never think, 'You've had your day. It's our time and our turn to fill the room.' This does little for their emotional, physical, mental and spiritual well-being. Jesus promised abundant life[45] without attaching a 'best-by date'.

It's time for those living life in the last lane to occupy the new room, to embrace the third act, and to climb the spiral staircase.

---

45. John 10:10.

Question marks!

- How would we live each day if the ageing process was perceived as an upward journey of spiritual renewal, rather than a downward spiral of no possibility?

- Describe how you might enrol your experience, expertise, knowledge and networking ability in a volunteer army to advance the kingdom of God.

- How do you plan to 'occupy' the additional space which an increased life expectancy might give you?

3

The Brooks Factor

Few films have the same popularity as *The Shawshank Redemption* (1994). Voted many viewers favourite film of all time, you would be hard pressed to find anyone who doesn't love this movie. With its redemptive storyline, hope and perseverance, it has over the decades become a timeless classic. Based on the writings of Stephen King, it tells the story of a banker Andy Dufresne (Tim Robbins) who is wrongly accused, charged and convicted of murdering his wife and her lover. Despite his claims of innocence, he is found guilty and sent to the notorious Shawshank State Penitentiary for life.

While movie-goers only have to live through the Shawshank experience for the two-hours, inmates had to learn how to survive sixty to seventy years in this dark, violent, oppressive, dictatorial and abusive environment. Imprisoned within this granite stronghold, Dufresne befriends a fellow inmate, an older man called Red (Morgan Freeman). Although the inter-play between these two principal inmates forms the backdrop to the whole movie, there is a collection of characters who together make this film an incredible piece of cinematography. One of those secondary characters is an inmate known as Brooks Hatlen (James Whitmore), or 'Brooksy' to his friends. Having served the whole of his adult life behind bars, Brooks is probably one of the saddest individuals who finds himself playing a key role in this Oscar-nominated movie. Characterising the dehumanising effects of long-term incarceration and how being ill-prepared for a life-changing transition can prove catastrophic. Unbeknown to James Whitmore, the character he portrays is something of a masterclass of life in the last lane that few of us can afford to ignore.

Transition which is often traumatic is made worse by the lack of planning and preparation. This is none more so than in that transitional moment when we step away from a full-time career into the realm of retirement. The need to find our reason for being in this moment is critical; without it, as in the case of Brooks, it could prove catastrophic.

Life is a journey involving numerous distractions, diversions and detours. To avoid getting lost we need a guidance system, a mindset that enables us to navigate our way through a terrain we have never travelled before.

Losing our way in life

We marvel at the modern gizmo called GPS, which in recent time has become the must-have accessory for cars, ships, airplanes, construction equipment, agricultural machinery, laptops and of course, the all-essential smartphone. Had the American government not released their Global Positioning System for civil use, the world may have remained directionally challenged for decades. Yet even those with a poor sense of direction must be comforted by the fact that scientists tell us that an implantable GPS device is not presently, technically feasible. But that said, medical science has recently discovered 'a type of brain cell known to help animals keep track of their location [which] has been found for the first time in humans . . . called grid cells . . . [they] tell a person where they are in their environment'.[46]

The question is, what happens when our internal guidance system fails? When, for reasons outside our control, we struggle to make sense of our surroundings and lose our way in life? When, overwhelmed by external forces, we begin to feel disorientated and confused? If this is reality, then perhaps it explains the difficult scenario facing one seventy-three-year-old parolee. A long-term prisoner recklessly released into the unknown. Without any sense of direction an elderly gentleman struggling to find his way in life, soon finds himself on a collision course with tragedy. Through a tragic set of circumstances, Brooks offers us a unique perspective on living life in the last lane.

Sentenced for a crime we are never told about, Brooks refers to himself as 'an old crook'. Having spent fifty years in prison, he had grown familiar with his surroundings. A small circle of friends became his surrogate family. Their camaraderie gave him a sense of belonging. And while prison routine gave him the structure and stability he so desperately needed, acting as prison librarian gave him a sense of purpose. Apart from the traumatic arrivals and tragic departures of Shawshank's inmates, little changed in Brooks' life. That is until the day of his release.

---

46. Tanya Lewis, 'Human Brains Have Internal GPS, Study Confirms', 9 August 2013, www.nbcnews.com (accessed 14.7.25).

All change

The biblical wisdom of King Solomon tells us that *change* will either bring the *best* or the *beast* out of us.[47] In Brooks' case, it was the latter. Confused and conflicted by his pending release, he took a knife and uncharacteristically threatened to kill a fellow inmate. Losing familiar landmarks at a phenomenal rate, his moral compass was beginning to malfunction. In his mind, committing murder would enable him to stay in the only safe and secure environment he knew – prison.

When later explaining Brooks' bizarre behaviour, a fellow inmate explained how having spent the whole of his adult life in prison, the thought of leaving terrified him. This journey into the unknown was something Brooks was totally ill-prepared for. Incarceration had become his lifestyle and institutionalism his mindset. But now everything was about to change!

All human life is metamorphic in nature. Transitioning from childhood to adulthood and then into elderhood is a change of seasons that inevitably involves physical, mental and social adjustment. While some are incremental, others are quantum leaps into the unknown. From the moment of birth, growing older is a factor of life and whether we like it or not, life's journey will require either minuscule or monumental changes.

Of all the transitional moments in life, stepping into elderhood is perhaps the most challenging. Elderhood, or what some have termed the 'third age'[48] is a stage of life in

---

47. Ecclesiastes 3.
48. Peter Laslett, *A Fresh Map of Life: The Emergence of the Third Age* (London: Weidenfeld & Nicolson, 1989).

which adults no longer work for financial reward, and their children have left home. Like Brooks, these retired empty-nesters are stepping into a season full of uncertainties. A time of life that is both undefined and potentially scary. Whatever age a person decides when leaving their career behind them, the first year is said to be the most dangerous.

Modern society places so much emphasis on *productivity*, that third agers are often valued for what they can or cannot do. Add *pace* or speed to this scenario, and we begin to see why seniors become disenfranchised from their community. When civilisation values a person according to their *pace* and *productivity*, then the narrative of those stepping into life's third act is to confront the challenge of change. How 'retired empty-nesters' navigate through this stage of life is first and foremost a matter of mental attitude. To maintain a high level of expectation in the face of all opposing factors is fundamental – a positive attitude being the antidote for fighting off the effects of age and the ageing process.

Cruelly stripped of the support and structure that prison life gave him, Brooks struggled to find his way in life. Ill-prepared for life on the outside, this elderly parolee found himself on a downward spiral of no possibility. When retirees step away from their workplace environment and the comfort and comradery it offered, that loss of purpose can be devastating. To step into the unfamiliar of retirement, with its lack of routine, structure and stability, can be disorientating.

Many of those who eagerly await retirement soon find the honeymoon period brief. Superseded by a season of disenchantment, it's only when new coping mechanisms are found that balance is restored.

Seeing red

Unable to adjust to life on the outside, Brooks expressed his feelings in a letter to his former inmates: 'Dear fellas, I can't believe how fast things move on the outside. I saw an automobile once when I was a kid, but now they're everywhere. The world went and got itself in a big damn hurry. I don't like it here. I'm tired of being afraid all the time. I've decided not to stay. I doubt they'll kick up any fuss. Not for an old crook like me.'

The harsh realities of his parole meant living in a halfway house and working as a bag boy in a local food store. Any positive thoughts Brooks had concerning his final years quickly dissipated. Unable to live through this terrifying nightmare, he carved a simple epitaph in the wooden beam of his lodgings that read, *'Brooks was here!'* before tragically crashing out of his earthly journey.

Scriptwriters had given both Brooks and Red the same musical notes with which to compose their own grand finale. Whereas one created a musical dirge, the other managed to compose a glorious dance. The difference being, one had hope, whereas the other didn't. As if to emphasis this fact, Andy Dufresne left Red a road map in the form of a letter reminding him that hope was a good thing, something that should never die.

As if to illustrate the importance of a workable guidance system, Red buys an old compass before setting off to find a town called Buxton. Refusing to allow a dreary house and dead-end job to define him, Red immortalises this transitional moment by carving his name next Brooks. The inscription now read: 'Brooks was here . . . So was Red.' Purpose-driven and guided by hope, Red makes his way from Buxton to a Mexican beach where his friend Andy awaits his arrival. Both men singing for the same song sheet, the lyrics of which read, *'Get busy living, or get busy dying.'*

Faced with partiality and prejudice, Third Agers need to maintain high levels of expectation in the face of all these opposing factors. Daily reminding themselves that there is a heavenly performance being played out in the earth, and no matter their pace or productivity they have a key role to play.

An inside job

In his book *Good to Great,* author Jim Collins describes a positive angle of approach to life as 'The Stockdale Paradox'. His phraseology is built around the story of Admiral Jim Stockdale, the highest-ranking United States military officer to be imprisoned in the infamous 'Hanoi Hilton'. Stockdale survived the Vietnam War, where others didn't. He puts his survival down to a faith that faced the facts. 'You must never confuse faith that you will prevail in the end – which you can never afford to lose – with the discipline to confront the most brutal facts of your current reality, whatever they might be.'[49] Old age is difficult and often demanding, but a mantra that faces up to such challenges is to 'Get busy living, or get busy dying'.

---

49. Jim Collins, *Good to Great* (New York: Random House, 2001), p. 85.

Without a well-adjusted angle of approach to life's third act, we will become incarcerated in a prison of our own making. As one well-known public speaker and blogger once wrote:

> It is possible to not only sentence ourselves to life without parole, but to place ourselves on a mental and emotional death row. We cannot get out on an appeal, because there is no judicial system holding us. We do not need a lawyer we just need to change the story in our head and leave. We have to change the narrative to truly leave our self-imposed prison, because the narrative in our head is our only jailer.[50]

Although Brooks was physically outside of prison, prison was not outside of him. Struggling to find his way in life, his freedom was fraught with emotional and social challenges. No matter how difficult or demanding our transition from adulthood to elderhood is, followers of Jesus Christ have the wherewithal to live free of those people, objects and events that seek to incarcerate them.

With its rigid structures, fixed traditions, controlling mechanisms, restrictive lifestyle and resistance to change, Shawshank is a clear example of institutional living. Prisons are places where uniformity is imposed and individuality is taken. Any social group can create a Shawshank culture: an environment in which abusive behaviour is practised and inmates go into survival mode, so as to find safety in numbers. Living under a dictatorial oversight, rules

---

50. Instagram, paulscanlonuk, Used with permission (accessed 3.6.25). Used with permission.

become paramount. Loud-mouthed inmates or overbearing guards lord it over those who show signs of weakness. Standardisation is the norm and imposed structures are king. Those daring to voice the need for change are quickly silenced. Here organisational mechanisms are used as mental straight-jackets. Well-rehearsed routines create a magnolia-coloured thinking. Together these things make for an environment that is bland and mind-blowingly boring. In this life-numbing atmosphere, positivity struggles to survive.

For those finding themselves on some kind of personal death row, suffering a life sentence without parole, God has in Christ unlocked the prison door but the handle is on the inside. No matter what stage of life we find ourselves, freedom belongs to those willing to give God access and by faith activate the redemptive work of Jesus Christ. To appropriate our freedom in Christ requires both a personal and corporate response.

In Peter's prison break, found in Acts 12, God miraculously opened the prison door and created a way of escape, but Peter's personal response was to 'dress [himself] and put on [his] sandals'.[51] Whereas, in the case of Lazarus being raised from the dead, he needed a community of friends to 'unbind him, and let him go'.[52] While Peter took personal responsibility to walk in the freedom God had made available, Lazarus needed a caring community to release him from the trappings of his former lifestyle.

---

51. Acts 12:8, ESV.
52. John 11:44, ESV.

Graveyards into gardens

Although sounding a little extreme, some local churches have for the elderly become nothing more than holding cells. Here third agers await their final sentencing. Put another way, churches can become philosophically like mortuaries in which the elderly are looked on as corpses awaiting burial. Rather than being released into meaningful activity, seniors are being restricted by the trappings of institutionalism. All this, when God raised his Son from the dead to show himself able to turn graveyards into gardens.

Rather than wandering aimlessly in the wild-open spaces of Christendom, the heavenly gardener wants to plant all believers into garden communities; local churches, in which Christians are cultivated in a way that enables them to grow into their God-given potential. Irrespective of age, ability, culture, gender, or social background, these garden centres are to become places where people are valued for who they are, not what they can or cannot do. Here the Head Gardener appoints under-gardeners to create an atmosphere conducive to spiritual growth. An environment in which seniors can reach a 'ripe old age' in the true sense of the phrase. Here spiritual saplings are watered and fed as anointed leaders set boundaries, weed out the cares of this world and when necessary, lovingly prune what is good, in order to produce what is best.

As a premier gardener, Adam was planted in a pre-prepared place. Within the Garden of Eden, he exercised the dual role of *governor* and *gardener*. Or as Moses writes, 'The LORD God took the man [Adam] and *put* him in the garden of Eden to *work it* and *keep it.*'[53] Purposefully positioned, God's first gardener had a specific assignment. His remit was to exercise a balance between the *organic* and *organised.* To be too organic would have created chaos, while becoming overly organised would have been too controlling. Exercising a balanced ambassadorial role in the world, Adam was called to establish an outpost of heaven on earth – a garden community. Here God's first family enjoyed the refreshing breeze of the Holy Spirit. Work became worship and relationships were rooted in the under-gardener enjoying a one-to-one with the Head Gardener on a daily basis.

To create twenty-first-century garden communities, Church leaders will need to recognise God's voice amidst a cacophony of worldly noise by giving quality time to the refreshing breeze of God's manifest presence.[54] In so doing servant-leaders will ensure that mere human activity does not sabotage their heavenly assignment.

God never intended these garden communities to become prison-like *greenhouses.* Clinically controlled environments in which people become 'pot-bound' and never get 'planted-out'. While spiritual seedlings need the greenhouse effect to develop a strong root system, once they are strong and secure in their faith, heaven's intention is to expose them to the world's elements. Here they are intended to blossom in such a way as to reflect the beauty of God's grace in all they say and do.

---

53. Genesis 2:15, ESV, emphasis mine.
54. Genesis 3:8.

Redeeming Shawshank

When man-made ideologies become set in stone, inmates will need to tunnel through the granite walls of institutionalism, to enjoy the 'freedom [by which] Christ has set [them] free'.[55] Institutionalism is perhaps one of the major challenges facing modern Christianity.

By creating a Shawshank environment, the herding instinct reigns supreme; tribalism, uniformity, cliques, controlling mechanisms, dictatorial leadership, uniformity and resistance to change become rampant.

When one-of-a-kind individuals enter the standardising mechanism of a local church, only to emerge the spitting image of the most charismatic inmate, something is seriously wrong. When 'mission-stations' become 'machine-shops', heavens desire to embroider the 'many-colored tapestry of God's grace' [56] soon unravels. Adopting a cookie-cutter approach to discipleship will ultimately extinguish what my old professor called 'The individuality of otherness'. Overly institutionalised churches remove individuality by placing originality on death row!

There are two sides to every argument. In his book *Christianity's Surprise*, C. Kavin Rowe writes of how:

Today we almost automatically think of institutions as bureaucratic extinguishers of vibrant faith and all that goes into them – dynamic relationships, power worship, works of justice and imaginative thinking. If you want to slow, or stop, the beating heart of new

---

55. Galatians 5:1.
56. 1 Peter 4:10, TPT.

64

faith, institutionalize it. If you want to oppress human beings, build institutions that smother their natural creativity. If you want to ensure that innovation never gets the upper hand, do things in an institution. If you want drudgery day after day, work in an institution.[57]

Anti-institutionalist thinkers point to the early Church and highlight the lack of organisational structure. But pro-institutionalists would argue that the early Church believed that the formation and transformation of the human heart required structure. To find a balance and a possible working solution to this institutional dilemma, Rowe blends a measure of both when speaking of early Christians as people who were 'institutionally creative'.[58] Local churches need structures, not straight-jackets.

Managing the miracle of spiritual growth requires individuals and corporations to use malleable wineskins. Structures able to cope with *an ever-changing world* while holding onto God's *never-changing word*. As keepers of the vineyard, twenty-first century leaders will need to become *'institutionally creative'* – imaginative couriers of the manifest presence of God. Men and women who march to a different drumbeat. Knowing that institutionalism is the breeding ground of injustice and unfairness they break with the status quo by refusing to create generational holding cells that incarcerate third agers.

The traditional view of all sixty-six-year-olds stepping blissfully into retirement is rapidly being dispatched to the

57. C. Kavin Rowe, *Christianity's Surprise* (Nashville, TN: Abingdon Press, 2020), Chapter 4, Institutions.
58. Ibid, Rowe.

history books. While some retirees are happy to slip silently into their autumn years, others want to speak out about institutional injustice and *get busy living* in the affairs of heaven on earth. Refusing to accept the stereotypical view of old age, this army of go-getting geriatrics are no longer willing to accept an ageist bubble. As Christian combatants, these radical retirees are subconsciously repeating the psalmist's plea, 'don't turn me out to pasture when I'm old or put me on the shelf when I can't pull my weight.'[59]

When third agers are thrown on the proverbial scrap heap by short-sighted, one-dimensional leaders, one is left wondering if ageism is alive and well. Because with an age-related problem about to peak, Christianity has to wake up and smell the coffee.

Breaking the age barrier

As Captain Charles 'Chuck' Yeager climbed into the cockpit of his purpose-built aircraft, he had only one thing on his mind. Not that this was any plane. With a fuselage shaped like a bullet, extremely thin wings built to overcome aerodynamic forces and a stabiliser to improve control, this experimental craft was built with one purpose in mind – speed.

As the American Air Force's most experience test pilot, Chuck Yeager was the ideal choice for this record-breaking mission. The fact that two days earlier he had broken two ribs by what he described as 'a disagreement with a horse' did nothing to discourage him from squeezing himself into

---

59. Psalms 71:8-11, *MSG*.

the cockpit. This was the opportunity of a lifetime, and he was not about to miss it. At 20,000 feet his aircraft was launched from the bomb-bay of a B-29 bomber and Yeager could begin his historic flight.

In a plane he affectionately named *Glamorous Glennis* after his wife, Yeager was about to take air travel to the next level. Although many thought an invisible 'barrier' made supersonic flight impossible and that the vibration alone would prove fatal, Yeager pushed through all opposing factors to achieve his goal.

On 14 October 1947, Captain Charles Yeager reached the speed of 700 miles per hour (Mach 1.06). In so doing he became the first person to break the sound barrier. Despite experiencing immense pressure, this pioneering pilot took flight to the next level and opened up the way for space travel.

In the light of an apparent age barrier, twenty-first-century Christianity needs breakthrough leaders 'to boldly go where no one has gone before'.[60] Men and women willing to ignore the pressure to conform to generational stereotypes and take godly risks to elevate the body of Christ to the next level. Refusing to take the easy option, these experimental leaders will open up new vistas and usher in a spiritual renaissance – a resurgence of intergenerational churches that truly reflect the purpose of heaven on earth.

In a world that idolises youth, the old are becoming increasingly invisible and irrelevant. Using phrases like 'Over the hill, 'Past their prime' 'Old Fogeys' and 'Spiritual dinosaurs', an older generation are increasingly feeling

---

60. From Paramount Television's *Star Trek: The Next Generation* (1987-94).

disenfranchised, devalued and discarded. Feeling surplus to requirements, both they and those who lead will need to find a way to break through those prejudicial ageist restrictions and create communities in which everyone, no matter what age, gender, race or culture, feel accepted, appreciated and approved. For if the traumatic transitioning of Brooks teaches us anything it is that:

- Neither our past or our present should dictate our future;

- A lack of purpose and hope will cause us to lose our way in life;

- When change happens, we will have to change with it;

- Third agers require garden rooms not spiritual graveyards;

- Freedom in Christ liberates us from any life sentence imposed by people, objects and events;

- Christianity needs pioneering leaders to break through the age barrier;

- Old age is a season to enjoy not endure;

- Finding our version of a Mexican beach in Zihuantanejo is paramount.

Question marks!

What are your thoughts regarding
the following statements:

- To imprison people in a system that limits them because of their age, gender, race or social background is a human typo in the divine narrative.

- An overly institutionalised church, is in danger of removing the diversity of individuality God intended.

- When 'silo-mentality' separates people according to age, we risk creating a mono rather than intergenerational church.

4

Scrapheap Challenge

Staring down at a mass of rusty car parts strewn all over the garage floor, I began to wonder if this was one restoration too far. Difficult to believe that this deconstructed mess was all that remained of a vehicle that once took pride of place in a London, West End car showroom. Attracted by its beautiful lines and reputation for reliability, some wealthy customer had parted with the equivalent of £43,000 ($53,000) to purchase what back then was a modern, pristine five-seater, open-top tourer. But time had not been kind. A hundred years of business, family and farm ownership had reduced this one-time pristine exhibit to something more suited to a scrapyard.

Custodians of vintage vehicles are faced with a dilemma. Fearing opposition from other road-users, some prefer to keep their prized possession in a temperature-controlled storage unit. Rarely seeing the light of day, these so-called 'trailer queens' will never again function in the way they were originally intended. Others might prefer to donate their vehicles to a museum. In so doing they not only create a visitors' attraction but confirm a commonly held belief that such outdated modes of transport have no place in a modern society.

In barns and backstreet garages the world over, enthusiasts spend countless hours attempting to breathe life back into rusty relics. While some tinker around the edges, ignoring any major mechanical issues, for the purist, originality is the holy grail of a true restoration. With no interest in refurbishment, their vision is to restore the vehicle back to what the original creator intended and beyond.

Attend any antique car concourse rally and it soon becomes clear that those true aficionados of automobile restoration go way beyond originality. By admiring the paint, upholstery, power unit and brightwork, spectators soon realise that a true restoration will result in a vehicle that looks, sounds and functions far better than it did when first leaving the production line.

Vision and vehicles

While marvelling at Henry Ford's genius in creating the first mass-market automobile, his resistance to change caused the company to lose its place as market leaders. By stubbornly maintaining the belief that customers could have any car they wanted, at an affordable price, as long as it was a soft-top Model T in black, would cost the Ford Motor Company dearly.

Staying faithful to the original *vision* does not mean we resist changing the *vehicle*. Amidst an ever-changing climate, General Motors went to war with Ford. Introducing

Scrapheap Challenge

the ability for customers to trade in their old vehicles, along with financial options, annual upgrades and a fully enclosed vehicle, GM succeeded on the back of Henry Ford's refusal to change. Admittedly, for a while the world was changing, and one man and his machine refused to change with it. In a matter of six years, Ford's 67 per cent share in the American Automobile market plummeted to 15 per cent.

Spiritualising the need for divine restoration alongside Henry Ford's resistance of change, author, speaker and podcaster Carey Nieuhoff states:

Churches who love the method more than the mission will die. It happened in the 1950's, in the 1970s, in the 1990s, and it's happening today. What was effective a decade ago isn't always effective today. Leaders who live in the past end up dying in the future.[61]

Many would argue that God's end-time vehicle, the Church, requires a full restoration. A spiritual process that brings back what is lost and in so doing creates something far better than the original. Time has not been kind to the Church. Used and abused by unscrupulous individuals, God's redeemed community is no longer functioning as the Creator originally intended. For those attempting to refurbish the Church while ignoring those underlying issues should remember that God's house is not a 'fixer upper' and papering over the cracks will do little to address those foundational issues.

---

61. Doug Paul, *Ready or Not: Kingdom Innovation for a Brave New World* (Washington DC: 100Mpublishing.com, 2002), p. xxxv.

73

Cosmetic cover-ups simply kick the ecclesiastical can down the road! To preserve the past by locking the body of Christ away in a sterilised environment may be one option. Another would be to create a museum piece to which members of the public are invited to attend at set times. Creating a visitors' attraction will only serve to confirm what many already believe, that an antiquated Church has no place in a modern society.

Art conservationists spend hours restoring and preserving an irreplaceable piece of art, one-of-a-kind masterpieces that convey the heart and soul of the original artist. Although a skilled craftsperson could create a pastiche of the same painting, a copy would fail to represent the Creator's original handiwork. 'God's masterpiece',[62] the Church, deserves more than a pastiche, it needs a divine work of restoration.

Unlike the dictionary definition, the biblical phrase 'to restore' means: *'To bring something back to the point at which its final state is far greater than the former.'* While human ingenuity could create a pastiche of the Church, such would lack the purpose, presence and power of the divine Creator.[63] God's end-time Church will be everything that first-century Christianity was, and more. It will be a supernatural inter-generational body of believers, that is without 'spot, or wrinkle'.[64] Lacking the spiritual *acne* of youth and the *wrinkles* of old age, the body of Christ will become an environment in which ageism is extinct.

62. Ephesians 2:10, NLT.
63. 2 Timothy 3:5, NIV.
64. Ephesians 5:27, KJV.

When it comes to handling an age-old problem, the policy of some leaders have is one of 'out with the old and in with new'. Disposing of anything that looks, smells or sounds old they inadvertently risk throwing the proverbial baby out with the bath water. Whereas, good stewards of the multicoloured grace of God – being conversant with the ways of the kingdom – behave 'like a master of a house, who brings out of his treasure what is new and what is old'.[65] Only by restoring a godly equilibrium will we rid the Church of partiality that values one generation above another. Leaders should not put themselves under pressure to accept what the elderly say just because of their age and experience, neither should they feel constrained to pursue the latest trends, just because the young are pushing for their inclusion.

Crisis of confidence

When it comes to the so-called 'longevity revolution' and the societies attitude towards it, something has to change. Too many third agers are experiencing a crisis of confidence and too few leaders seem aware of it. When a church adopts a *first-half-of-life culture,* resources tend to flow in one direction. While pouring time, energy and resources into children, youth and family ministry is commendable, to ignore the world's fastest growing demographic, an ageing population, is deplorable.

A former Archbishop of Canterbury was asked in a media interview to describe how he saw the Church today. His

---

65. Matthew 13:52, ESV.

response was that 'he hoped that the Church would grow progressively younger. The Church today seemed to him rather like a very old grandmother, who sat by the chimney-breast muttering to herself, ignored by the rest of the family and out of touch with its culture'.[66] While understanding the archbishop's concern regarding ageing congregations, one has to wonder if there's not some elements of ageism in his comments.

The World Health Organization defines ageism as the 'stereotypes (how we think), prejudice (how we feel), and discrimination (how we act) towards others or oneself based on age'.[67] By their reckoning, one in two people are ageist. Whether it's employment, governmental policies, medical or social care, many seniors feel isolated, ignored and somewhat irrelevant. Surrounded by such prejudicial thinking, the Church has to become a leading light in restoring well-balanced, ageless communities. To cultivate garden rooms in which all generations live and learn together in an atmosphere of generational equality. Feeling cast aside in favour of a younger model, many seniors feel as if they have been thrown on the proverbial scrap heap. This knowingly or unknowingly happens to an older generation when we:

- Ignore their existence;

- Abuse their kind-heartedness;

- Refuse to accept their valid contribution;

---

66. https://viamedia.news/2018/02/23/is-the-church-of-england-guilty-of-ageism/ (accessed 24.7.25).
67. Ageing: Ageism www.who.int (accessed 24.7.25).

- Treat their wisdom, knowledge, expertise and experience as irrelevant;

- Forget to celebrate significant anniversaries;

- Create a first-half-of-life culture;

- Treat third agers as invisible;

- Fail to ask or think how in-house changes will affect seniors;

- Refuse to give retirees quality listening time;

- Take on society's stereotypical view of senior citizens;

- Treat retirees in a condescending manner;

- Marginalise and exclude older people from the community;

- Bypass a gifted individual on the basis of age, rather than ability.

Speaking of this generational dilemma, Winston Churchill said:

One of the signs of a great society is the diligence with which it passes culture from one generation to the next. This culture is the embodiment of everything the people of that society hold dear: its religious faith, its heroes ... When one generation no longer esteems its own heritage and fails to pass the torch to its children, it is saying in essence that the very foundational principles and experiences that make the society what it is are no longer valid. This, of course, leaves that next generation without any sense of definition or direction, making them the fulfilment of Karl Marx's dictum, "A people without a heritage are easily persuaded".

What is required when this happens and the society has lost its way is for leaders to arise who have not forgotten the discarded legacy and who love it with all their hearts. They can then become the voice of that lost heritage, wooing an errant generation back to the faith of their fathers, back to the ancient foundations and bedrock values and traditions.[68]

God's generals are going home

With the recent passing of so many spiritual giants,[69] we are witnessing the end of an era. God's generals are going home and a changing of the guard is taking place. These former Titans of Truth invested their lives in restoring the Church. They were known as Kingdom Innovators, who refused to allow those non-biblical boundaries set by a previous generation to limit them. As godly inspired thinkers, they knew that 'what becomes inflexible . . . eventually [becomes] irrelevance'.[70] With their passing, one has to wonder who will rise up to take their place? Who will step in to motivate the next generation to go further than the previous one? Maybe the answer in part lies in recognising and releasing those ageing pacesetters,

68. Stephen Mansfield, *Never Give In: The Extraordinary Character of Winston Churchill* (Devon: Highland Books, 1995), pp 190-191.
69. Tim Keller, David Pytches, George Verwer, Charles Stanley, Rosalyn and Jimmy Carter, Jack Hayford, Loren Cunningham, Dick Iverson, Kevin J. Conner, Frank Damazio to name but a few.
70. Paul, *Ready or Not*, p. xxxiv.

who at present stand idly by watching from the sidelines of most local churches. Given the opportunity, an older generation could inspire and instruct a younger generation in the ways of God.

Time is running out on this ready-made school of mentors. Third agers are sadly having to watch their younger counterparts make the same mistakes they did. And as long as seniors are expected to sit silently in the corner of church activities, a library of wisdom, experience and expertise is going to waste.

> The history of God's people is marked by innovators and pioneers in all sectors of society. It's in our lifeblood. In fact, the last two thousand years paints an astonishing picture of followers of Jesus innovating in social movements, art, technology, architecture, biological sciences, church life, psychological development, movement multiplication (and that's barely scratching the surface). And yet today, rather than being on the forefront of innovation, both within and outside of church life, Western Christianity seems stuck ... In the world in which we now live, the people of God either need to innovate or simply close up shop and stop fighting a war of attrition.[71]

Where are today's apostolic pioneers who refuse to get bogged down in the quagmire of earth's gravitation pull? Where are those inspired innovators, who will build inter-generationally? For by creating a culture in which believers

---

71.   Paul, *Ready or Not*, p. xxvii.

care for, work with and learn from people of all ages, Christianity will become a beacon of hope in a dark and dreary world.

Is the Church ageist?

In a recent statement made by the charitable organisation Faith in Later Life, it was stated that: 'In churches, the proportion aged 80+ has doubled or even tripled in the last 10 years. Across the denominations, this brings great opportunities for church – to nurture, develop and value these members, to bring glory and give service to the kingdom of God.' A generation that should be viewed as 'a gift to enjoy, rather than a burden to bear'.[72]

If seniors are to become rightfully involved in the life of every local church, then hard questions need to be asked. Because if we falter now, we will fail one of the largest and fastest growing demographics on the planet. So perhaps, now is the time to ask the question: 'Is ageism alive and well in the Church?' In characterising this dreadful blight on society, some would argue that:

- When the elderly are *harassed* by ageist jokes, insults or off-handed remarks – then *ageism is present*.

- To encounter *exclusion,* whereby seniors are intentionally left out of group discussion or activities, sidelined and having no *involvement*

---

72. www.faithinlaterlife.org/does-my-church-value-older-people (accessed 14.7.25).

or considered part of the team – then *ageism is prevalent.*

- When seniors are denied the opportunity to share their wisdom, experience, expertise and knowledge accrued over the years – then *ageism is problematic.*

- When organisations treat third agers in a way that is *infantile*, speaking to them as children, making them feel humiliated and frustrated – then *ageism has become a pandemic.*

Ageism is 'based on deeply ingrained, negative stereotypes of what old people are really like, ageism is used to rationalize discrimination and to confuse our discussions about rights and privilege'.[73] Like racism, ageism needs to be called out for what it is. Discrimination of any kind is both hurtful to those involved and harmful to the ongoing purposes of God.

To drill down into a churches culture regarding ageism, perhaps we should ask . . .

- Do those on your platform or in the pulpit reflect an inter-generational community?

- How age-relative is your welcoming team?

- Does your worship philosophy represent an intergenerational or one-generational mindset?

---

73. 'Is Your Church Ageist', www.umcdiscipleship.org, 2 October 2006 (accessed 14.7.25).

- Are the over sixty-fives given a voice into your present church leadership team?

- When was the last time an over fifty-five-year-old candidate was shortlisted for a paid or unpaid church vacancy?

- Does your diversity, equality and inclusion policy address ageism?

- How do you actively serve, support and assimilate third agers into your church?

- Is a silo-mentality locking seniors into an age-related bubble?

- How and when do young people engage with an older generation?

- Are your buildings, programmes, timings and commitments senior-friendly?

- Have you created a first-half-of-life culture that focuses primarily on children, youth and family ministries?

- When was the last time a senior citizen was invited to a youth gathering to share their faith story?

- Does your applied preaching take an older generation into consideration?

- Do you infantile your conversation when speaking to the elderly?

- How are you intentionally drawing on the wisdom, experience, expertise, knowledge and networking ability, of those enjoying life's third act?

Last lane living is made more challenging by people operating with an ageist agenda. If their stereotypical thinking was only confined to government, business, social and medical care, that would be bad enough, but sadly this insipid belief system has seeped into Christian communities. Being robbed of their self-worth and stripped of their dignity, third agers are fast becoming casualties of a youth-obsessed culture. Left hurting and abandoned beside the roadside of life, only a Samaritan spirit[74] can bring healing and restoration. For while *thermometer* type leaders might state the obvious, only *thermostat* people will alter the atmosphere.

Spotters and stonemasons

If the theory of gravity came to Sir Isaac Newton while sitting under an apple tree, we should not be surprised when lightbulb moments happen in the strangest of circumstances. In the case of assistant TV producer Eve Kay, the idea for a new television game show came while watching the movie *Apollo 13.* Her moment of pure genius came for the scene in which NASA engineers had a limited time in which to construct a carbon dioxide filter from the parts available onboard the crippled lunar space capsule. This cinematic scenario, became the basis of a TV game show known in the UK as *Scrapheap Challenge,* and in the US as *Junkyard Wars.*

The basic idea of this unique TV game show involved two teams of four or five contestants competing against the

---

74.   Luke 10:25-37.

clock and each other. Set inside a large industrial scrapyard, each team was given ten hours to complete a specific challenge. Using only those parts found in the junkyard, each programme was built around a different challenge. From building a car crusher to creating a machine that could fling a British Leyland Mini as far as possible, this show soon became a firm family favourite. Each episode was built around a simple premise: Using the expertise of your team, build a specified working machine in the time allocated, using only discarded items that others have deemed redundant.[75]

With the blast of an airhorn, the challenge began. While some team members remained at their base discussing the build, two were given a different assignment. Acting as *spotters*, these two eagle-eyed team players raced around the scrapyard on four-wheel-drive quadbikes, along with a suitable trailer in tow. Their specific task, to find those redundant items necessary to complete the build.

Besides their freedom to ride quadbikes at break-neck speed around an almost deserted scrapyard, these hunter-gatherer types are driven by a desire to:

- Engage in a process of restoration;

- See usefulness in what others deem useless;

- Connect with the disconnected;

- Recycle what others have made redundant;

- Find treasure where others see trash.

75.   Discovery Channel, Channel 4.

Without appearing overly simplistic, what if local churches began to engage people as *pastoral spotters* and *prophetic stonemasons*? Let me explain. The present 'Scrapheap Challenge' facing local churches regarding third agers could be partially remedied by recognising and releasing pastoral and prophetic individuals. This would involve engaging spiritually mature Christ followers whose 'Modus Operandi' is to engage with the disengaged. The antithesis of consumeristic *'getters'*, these people are *'givers'*. Their role is to scan the congregation, before and after any corporate gathering looking for in this case 'elderly edge-people' who clearly want to become more engaged.

Every local church needs its back row, a place where those who, for one reason or another, need time and space before re-engaging. Yet whenever a vibrant, growing church gathers, there is always the possibility of people on the periphery. And some of those will be third agers, who long to become an integral part of the whole.

As some local churches move away from a pastoral towards a CEO leadership style, visionary leaders cannot afford to adopt tunnel vision that ignores those on the edges.

Offering more than a solitary handshake and well-rehearsed Christianise greeting, these *pastoral spotters* have no desire to be superficial. Spending quality time, they want to truly engage with periphery people. With a passion to see the solitary set into families[76] they, more than anyone, understand the principle that 'new wine is found in the cluster'.[77] Their goal is to transition the disenfranchised

76. Psalm 68:6, paraphrased.
77. Isaiah 65:8.

from the outer edges into the centre, to see the solitary set into God's family so as to experience the new wine of God's Holy Spirit. Working tirelessly, these individuals are seeking to create a Christian construct that the apostle Paul described as 'the whole body, joined and held together by every supporting ligament, grows and builds itself up in love, as each part does its work'.[78]

Being part of a crowd rather than belonging to a community is one of the greatest challenges facing performance-based churches.

The iconic pattern of ancient drystone walls criss-crossing the English countryside is recognised as one of the most distinctive agricultural landscapes in Western Europe. Believed to be some of the oldest man-made structures in existence, these walls subdivide farmland and protect livestock. Using local stone, masons construct these stony masterpieces without any adhesive agent. To observe these artisans at work is to watch an artist lovingly and continually picking up and putting down a particular stone, all with the intention to get to know it's idiosyncrasies. By appreciating the stone's size, shape, strengths and weaknesses, a stonemason has the ability to find the best fit for each one-of-a-kind rock. Whereas some will become a foundation stone, others through stones, capstones or infill – every uniquely shaped stone will find its place and function.

---

78. Ephesians 4:16, NIV.

Appreciating the unappreciated, the role of a *prophetic stonemason* in a disconnected society has never been more necessary. Able to see beyond the immediate into God's ultimate, these spiritual individuals operate with God's grace and gentleness. Their mission is to pick up one-of-a-kind 'living stones'[79] and enable them to find their fit within that magnificent edifice called the Church.[80]

Those who emphasise uniformity over diversity build with a Babylonian mindset. Building his egotistic tower, King Nimrod convinced the people of Babylon to build a tower that reached to the heavens. Arrogantly stating, 'Come, let's make bricks and bake them thoroughly.' This meant

---

79.   1 Peter 2:4-12.
80.   Ephesians 2:19-22, NASB.

that, 'They used bricks instead of stone, and bitumen for mortar.'[81] As a spiritual master builder, the apostle Paul clearly stated to the church in Ephesus that 'you also, like living stones, are being built into a spiritual house' to glorify God.[82] Without being set into God's spiritual house, living stones will become isolated, vulnerable and lacking in purpose.

Recognising and responding to the uniqueness of otherness in people is what makes prophetic stonemasons essential. To standardise all seniors is like saying all carpenters, mechanics or surgeons are the same, simply because of their title. Not all 'retirees' want to be placed into a 'retirement group' where well-rehearsed stories and a catalogue of ailments are shared on a regular basis. For the sake of maintaining their sanity, some would much prefer to converse with people half their age.

To build inter-generational communities church leaders would be advised to consider the role and responsibility of *pastoral spotters* and *prophetic stonemasons*.

I dreamed a dream

The name Susan Boyle has, in recent years, become synonymous with the phrase, 'Don't judge a book by its cover!' Brazenly stepping onto the stage to audition for the 2009 TV Talent show *Britain's Got Talent*, few gave her a chance of getting through to the next stage, let alone taking second place in the final. Acting and appearing much older

---

81. Genesis 11:3-4, NIV.
82. 1 Peter 2:1-8, NIV.

than she actually was, first appearances were deceptive. While only in her late forties, her dress and demeanour was that of someone much older. Still living in her family home in West Lothian, Scotland, she was clearly moving outside her comfort zone. Although having been a singer from age of twelve, at the age of forty-seven she was stepping from the sidelines of obscurity into a crucible full of critics. Although confessing a desire to be the next Elaine Paige, few gave her much hope. As the judges rolled their eyes and the audience seemed incredulous, the signal was given to begin the backing track. Her song of choice was the iconic, 'I Dreamed a Dream' from the hit Broadway musical *Les Misérables*.

From her first note cynicism disappeared, as she stunned the judges and wowed the audience. While others tried to mentally sideline her, Susan Boyle refused to let anyone dismiss her dream. Proving once again that no matter the stage of life we find ourselves, or whether we fully appreciate the giftings of God has given us, our angle of approach will mean that we either soar or step onto a downward spiral of no possibility.

As the world's population gets older, third agers are now seeing that they have a key role in the affairs of heaven on earth. And while some retirees may prefer to spend their time relaxing at home pursuing their hobbies, others are looking for a more adventurous way of life. Living life in the last lane proposes a very different vision for an age traditionally associated with withdrawal and even passivity. The challenge for an older generation is to stop allowing people and events to throw them onto the proverbial scrapheap and likewise for Christian leaders to incorporate those others have made redundant.

Question marks!

- What is the oldest vehicle you have ever owned and would you swap it for your present mode of transport?

- If ageism marginalises people from the local church, how could a 'Good Samaritan' type person help?

- Could you ever see yourself as a *pastoral spotter* or a *prophetic stonemason*, if so, how do you intend to make this a reality?

- Susan Boyle had a dream, so when it comes to being involved in the affairs of heaven on earth, what would your dream be?

5

The Ninth Seat

As a quintessential British sporting event, 'The Boat Race' is a race of rivals fought between two of the world's oldest universities. Advertised as the world's longest surviving sporting challenge, this gruelling four-and-a-quarter-mile river race demands the stamina of a marathon runner and the guts of a prize fighter. Crewed by amateurs, each full-time university student commits to six months of blood, sweat and tears for the chance to compete in an annual rowing race that lasts about seventeen minutes.

Established in 1828, the Cambridge University Boat Club lives and breathes for the opportunity to beat its rival, Oxford. An Oxford-educated Cambridge don named Mark de Rond spent a whole year observing the Cambridge squad. In his book *The Last Amateurs* he speaks of this battle royal as being a contest between world-class sportsmen, and while taking part is everything, the agony of losing is unimaginable.

Using slim carbon fibre reinforced racing boats known as shells, a worldwide audience of millions watch two competing crews race with the incoming tide of London's

Thames River. When analysing the inner workings of the Cambridge crew, de Rond writes:

> Eight of these are caught up in one of the most painful endurance sports imaginable for 4 miles and 374 yards on a whimsical, coffee-coloured course; the rowing requires not just cardiovascular fitness but enormous will-power to be able to push oneself through successive pain barriers. It's a vehicle for exploring the outer limits of human performance, where the two crews will row alongside each other until one of them decides it can no longer win.[83]

While 80 per cent of this race depends on an eight-man crew, the remaining 20 per cent is down to the person occupying the ninth seat. Although their value is often queried, the so-called coxswain or cox can make or break a team. Choosing the right man or woman for this seat is crucial! As the only forward-facing member of the crew, the person occupying the ninth seat will have to navigate through formidable waves, bitter winds and tidal influences. With a band of fast-flowing water barely wide enough for two boats to race side by side, the coxswain fights for the preferred line around three large bends. All the while steering the boat with a rudder the size of a credit card.

From the number one 'stroke' who sets the pace, through the powerhouse of rowers three to six, to the 'bow' whose blade makes the most difference in terms of direction and stability, the one who occupies the ninth

---

83. Mark de Rond, *The Last Amateurs* (London: Icon Books, 2008), p. 9.

seat is the brains of the boat. Constantly shouting words of encouragement, they fulfil a role of captain, coach, cheerleader, communicator and when necessary, a calming influence on those striving for stroke perfection. As the only non-rower their position is one of great influence; their power, though immense, depends on their ability to make others powerful. The role of the person in the ninth seat is to awaken possibility in every member of the crew. Although a physical lightweight, their presence can make the difference between winning and losing. While not for the faint-hearted, the coordinated effort of the coxswain could be simply stated as: to *steer* and to *cheer*.

Don't fit in!

Whether it's within the family, church or society at large, many third agers struggle to fit in. Feeling like an uninvited guest at a public event has become something of an occupational hazard for the elderly. Ignored, isolated and invisible, many seniors are increasingly being made to feel unwanted and uncared for.

Today we think nothing of seeing an iconic poster of Elvis Presley plastered on a wall. As the so-called 'King of Rock and Roll' he is regarded as one of the most significant cultural figures of the twenty-first century music scene. Generally speaking, we would consider him to be an extremely popular individual. But the truth is Elvis was different and initially he struggled to fit into his surroundings. Those who knew him in his early years would say that he looked, acted, moved and sounded different. Author and writing coach Dan Blank writes:

It's shocking to hear again and again how Elvis didn't fit in anywhere. How he dressed was wildly different from everyone else around him. How he would walk in a room or on stage or into group setting, and people just didn't know what to think. He often wore pink and black ... He was shy, and didn't fit into conversation easily.[84]

Fearing isolation and loneliness there is for older people a pressure to conform – to camouflage their real self in order to blend into their surroundings. In an ever-changing world, nothing is more important than to maintain the essence of who we really are. Especially for those who confess to be Christ followers for 'if any person is [ingrafted] in Christ (the Messiah) he is a new creation (a new creature altogether); the old [previous moral and spiritual condition] has passed away. Behold, the fresh and new has come!'[85] Within this new-creation framework, it's vital that no matter our age or stage of life, we live with godly acceptance and authenticity.

To be hidden in what could prove to be our finest hour is not the life God intended. For in that majestic mosaic called life, there is a perfect fit for everyone. So perhaps we should prayerfully consider what it means for us to occupy the ninth seat.

84. Dan Blank, 'Don't fit in', https://wegrowmedia.com/don't-fit-in/, 2022 (accessed 14.7.25).
85. 2 Corinthians 5:17, AMPC.

The ninth seat

The phrase 'A picture is worth a thousand words' speaks of the impact of visual communication. Although art is subjective, certain pictures can stir the emotions more effectively than words alone.

Having presented a verbal depiction of the Oxford/Cambridge Boat Race, it could be argued that there is a much larger landscape lurking behind this nautical narrative; like some art restorer finding another masterpiece hidden beneath the surface – a ghostly image not immediately apparent to the naked eye.

Welcome to the world of prophetic imagery!

Using broad brush strokes, this chapter is a visual aid, creating an inspirational image of a forward-looking third ager occupying a God-ordained version of the ninth seat; a divine placement for which seniors are well-suited. For if this quintessential British sporting event was an allegory, the boat would represent the three God-inspired institutions of the family, the Church and the nation. And while the crew would speak of those working incredibly hard in all three areas, the coxswain would speak of those spiritual veterans willing to take their place in *steering* and *cheering* those involved in the race of their lives.

With an incoming tide of social influencers seeking to drive those God ordained institutions off course, there is an urgent need for seniors to occupy the ninth seat. To abdicate their divine placement would make them equivalent to the biblical David, who vacated his seat at the king's table for fear of an insecure and somewhat threatening leadership.[86] To hide from a spear-throwing Saul, while understandable, is like an older generation cowering in the company of overbearing leaders. For us to miss out on our God-given placement would be a mistake of gargantuan proportion.

When a literal storm sought to scupper the disciples' boat, Jesus stood from a position of rest and stilled those external elements that were threatening God's revealed will on earth. Just as the risen, glorified Christ occupies a heavenly seat from which he dispenses godly authority – those seniors who see themselves as being seated with Christ 'in the heavenly places in Christ Jesus'[87] have through faith the wherewithal to exercise spiritual authority in whatever setting they find themselves. Here, then, is a loving heavenly Father calling seniors to 'Please, take your seats as the performance of a lifetime is about to begin'.

For third agers to occupy the ninth seat, it will require them becoming . . .

---

86. 1 Samuel 20:25.
87. Ephesians 2:6.

Forward seers

Just as their natural counterparts are the only person in the boat to be forward-facing, those occupying a godly version of the ninth-seat must have anointed vision to see supernaturally what cannot be seen naturally.

As we scale the spiral staircase of life, our 360-degree perspective is enlarged. With increased hindsight, insight and foresight, seniors are well-suited to see things from a different perspective. Refusing to live with a rear-view mirror perspective and nostalgically hold on to the past, ninth-seaters are set on pursing God's preferred future. To lack a God-anointed vision for families, churches and society at large, will be detrimental for anyone seeking to fulfil their God-given assignment. Unlike the rest of the crew, the coxswain must by reason of their seating be forward-looking. For they, like us, are called to live the immediate in the light of an ultimate. To steer a straight course without deviation or hesitation.

When asked what motivated the creator of the *Star Wars* movies, it's rumored that George Lucas answered: 'I caught a glimpse of the future and decided to go there!' If true, that would make him a classic forward-thinker. Someone who fosters a flexible mindset able to expand beyond those present man-made boundaries. Or as DeVern Fromke in his book *Unto Full Stature* puts it:

In each generation God always has had those men [and women] whose framework of vision reached beyond the general consciousness to see God's larger purpose. They lived and breathed with a divine destiny consciousness imparted by God. Such [persons] always moved beyond the narrow vision of their day.[88]

Those who occupy the ninth-seat are by natural forward-facing visionaries. Refusing to take on board the classic backward-looking, nostalgic, golden-oldies type thinking, they are 'forgetting what is behind and straining towards what is ahead'.[89] Having a progressive mindset, the past merely becomes a means to propel them into God's preferred future. For those spiritual Luddites who refuse to accept God-ordained change, they risk missing out on life as God intend.

With an adverse head-wind trying to blow families, churches and nations off course and a demonic tsunami threatening to scupper these vessels, seniors cannot afford the luxury of spectating from the sidelines. As the only forward-looking member of the crew, those occupying the ninth seat need anointed eyesight to see what lies ahead. Like some twenty-first-century version of an Old Testament prophet, they need the ability to see what is coming down the track and encourage others to act accordingly. To merely see and state the obvious is no longer amenable for the ongoing purpose of God. Society does not need more *echoes* repeating what everyone else in the room is saying. It needs people like John the Baptist who living in total dependance on God became 'a *voice* [crying] In the wilderness'.[90] Society needs *voices* not *echoes*. Living at a pivotal point in history, John became a hinge on which

---

88. DeVern Fomke, *Unto Full Stature* (Seminole, FL: Sure Foundation, 1965), p. 39.
89. Philippians 3:13, NIV.
90. Isaiah 40:3, emphasis mine.

the past, present and God's preferred future swung. A person who valued God's unchanging Word in an ever-changing world.

For third agers to occupy the ninth-seat they will need to become . . .

Forward speakers

Just as the Old Testament style of leadership took on a dualist role of prophet and king (the monarchy listening to the voice of the prophet who could see what was happening around them and coming down the track), one has to wonder if twenty-first-century Christianity has so elevated the role of 'kingly leadership' that we have inadvertently silenced the prophetic voice.

The first coming of Jesus Christ was prefaced by the appearance of John the Baptist, a prophetic voice crying in the wilderness.[91] One has to wonder if the second coming of our Lord will only be made possible by reinstating the prophetic voice being spoken in families, churches and nations alike. Not some operational gift confined to corporate Christian gatherings, but prophetic third agers lovingly chatting with parents, church leaders and those working in society. With a lifetime of experience, expertise, wisdom and knowledge, God is looking for a return on that investment by seniors occupying the ninth seat and thereby becoming those who *steer* and *cheer* those around them.

Even a casual glance at history tells us that older people have tended to trash the young. The ancient Greeks

---

91. John 1:23.

99

complain about their children being disrespectful and having disgusting eating habits. Roman playwrights often incorporated a central theme of a disapproving father and a delinquent son. In the first century AD, Seneca the Elder wrote, 'Our young men have grown slothful. Their talents are left idle, and there is not a single honourable occupation for which they will toil night and day.'[92] The Renaissance writers complained about noisy youths singing rude songs in inappropriate places. Some scholars actually believe that Mao Zedong's Cultural Revolution was rooted in an older generation fearing that a younger generation had grown soft and lacked the experience of past revolutionaries. All of which serves to confirm the fact that the old criticising the young is something all generations have had to contend with! However, seeking to arbitrate between these two warring factions, Jason Feifer, editor-in-chief of *Entrepreneur* magazine, encourages us to: 'Look around: Everything we know – everything we have ever relied upon, or been impressed by, or adored, or treasured, or desired – was created by a generation who had been dismissed by the one before it.'[93]

So maybe it's time to change the narrative, for third agers to stop being overly protective of the past and fearful for the future; to start believing that their younger counterparts will shine brighter, build better and reach further, than they ever did. To write this new chapter, seniors will need to become speakers of possibility, rather than prophets of doom.

92. https://gen.medium.com/why-older-people-have-always-trashed-young-people-8f918529009a (accessed 24.7.25).
93. https://gen.medium.com/why-older-people-have-always-trashed-young-people-8f918529009a (accessed 24.7.25).

The young may do things differently, but rather than pulling them down, they need to be built up. We all learn through our mistakes, and those with a long list of life experiences should perhaps look back and remember their own catalogue of catastrophic errors before criticising others. Insisting on perfection will inadvertently ostracise an older generation from a younger audience.

Jeering comes in various guises. From a visual show of disrespect to a more vocal shout of disgust, people air their personal views in a variety of ways. But no matter the format, jeering is a gross misrepresentation of the Father heart of God. As a loving Father, God took every opportunity to cheer his Son. At his baptism and amidst the brilliance of his transfiguration, the Father is heard saying, 'This is my beloved Son, in whom I am well pleased.'[94] Not that his praise reverberated for his Son's *performance*, but heaven's applause was based on his Son's *position*. Before Jesus ever performed a miracle or preached a sermon, his Father took the opportunity to speak words of acceptance, appreciation and approval.

A fatherless generation is an ever-growing crisis affecting millions of young people. Those embroiled in this negative environment struggle to develop socially, emotionally, spiritually and academically. Feeling insecure, the young are desperately searching for adults who will give them affirmation. Operating out of an 'Orphan Spirit',[95] they feel 'Withheld From' and as such create an 'Entitlement Generation,' that believes 'Life Owes Them'. Against this

---

94. Matthew 3:15-17, ESV.
95. Orphan Spirit – a state of mind, which through no fault of their own, a person feels abandoned, rejected, lonely and lacking a sense of belonging. Struggling with trust issues, they feel as if they do not fit in.

backdrop, even the sons and daughters of God have become somewhat reticent to step onto the stage of world events, let alone take on a speaking role. For these precious people, the last thing they need is the cynicism of their elders. To behave badly towards a younger generation is both demoralising and destructive!

Although certain sections of society view seniors as spiritual lightweights and question their value, in occupying the ninth seat, we question the validity of their perspective. To abdicate this role will not only set families, churches and society at large adrift, but in so doing, create a rudderless generation. So how do third agers position themselves to *steer* and *cheer* when so much of today's society ignores their potential value?

Ageless advice

For those who see themselves as Christ followers and 'partakers of the divine nature',[96] becoming 'incarnational' should be second nature to them. For just as 'The Word became flesh and blood, and moved into the neighborhood',[97] seniors need to position themselves in a way that brings heaven to earth. Even when others seek to sideline you as they did the incarnate Christ, unless God directs you otherwise, be present in the moment.

Even when leaders fail to set you a place at the table, as an ambassador of heaven on earth you have the legal right to be present. While others fail to appreciate your expertise,

---

96.   2 Peter 1:4, NASB.
97.   John 1:14, MSG.

experience, wisdom and knowledge, third agers cannot afford to be absent without leave. Whether a family event, a church gathering or some kind of community forum, if invited, see that setting as a God-given sphere of influence and do so by following two simple principles. Firstly to:

- **Turn up.** Whatever space we are invited to occupy, we should be present in the moment. To be *physically* there is never enough, we need to *mentally* and *spiritually* occupy the space. Even when faced with the most challenging and diverse environments, our modius operandi must be, 'If God wants me there, I want to be there.'

  When a decision is made to remove someone from the field of play, simply on the basis of age not ability, a host of negative attitudes attempt to rob us of our joy and sense of well-being. But faced with this kind of situation we should perhaps take pointers from a former English professional footballer.

  In the summer of 2003, David Beckham moved from his beloved Manchester United to Real Madrid. Following a series of defeats and various team managers, an Italian hardliner by the name of Fabio Cappello was appointed as Real Madrid's new manager. For reasons only known to Fabio, his first decision as head coach was to bench two of his star players, Ronaldo and Beckham.

  To say Beckham was annoyed would be an understatement. Yet while being forced to spectate his team, an opportunity to play American soccer became available. When hearing of the offer,

Cappello took Beckham aside and told him in no uncertain terms that he would not play for his team again. Being wrongly accused of instigating a conversation with the Americans was bad enough, but worse was to come. At the next team training session, the manager cruelly told Beckham to move to the sidelines, well away from the team. From now on he would have to train alone.

Seeing the writing was on the wall, Beckham had to decide how he would handle this critical moment. Having six months left on his contract, a speedy exit was impossible. With the possibility of never being able to train or play with Real Madrid again, a negative reaction would be understandable. But that was not Beckham's style. Whenever the team was training, he would train with a trainer on the sidelines. When his team was playing, he would cheer from the bench. When someone eventually asked why he acted this way, his response was that even though he wasn't wanted, he wanted to be there.[98]

When organisational leaders bench third agers solely on the basis of age not ability, we can either react negatively or respond positively. Rather than adopting a mental or physical opting-out policy, we need by God's grace to say to ourselves, 'Even though I'm not wanted, I want to be here.' Because being present in the moment is the prerequisite for a divine encounter. For although insecure leaders

---

98. *Beckham*, Netflix documentary series, 2023.

might refuse to draw on our wisdom, we should remember that in God's economy, silence is golden.

When visiting a neighbour's spotless home with our brood of lively youngsters, the situation was fraught with possible behavioral challenges. Having being shown into a spotless lounge where there was a Dralon-covered three-piece suite that you only had to breathe on to make the perfectly brushed pile appear out of shape, and watching our youngest make a bee-line for the sofa, my wife speedily caught their eye and directed them to sit elsewhere. All without saying a word. It was like watching a parental miracle in motion. Perhaps that is what the psalmist was talking about when he wrote, 'I will instruct you and teach you in the way you should go; I will counsel you with my loving eye on you.'[99] In some situations our silence can speak louder than words.

The reality is, 'salt' preserves without making a sound, and 'light' exposes the darkness without making a noise. While thermometers merely measure the temperature, thermostats change the atmosphere – be the latter.

- **Tune in.** Just as a Coxswain grips a string in either hand to steer the boat with a rudder the size of credit card, those who occupy God's ninth seat need not only to embrace God's Word, but partner with the person of God's Holy Spirit.[100]

---

99. Psalm 32:8, NIV.
100. Philippians 2:1.

When the New Testament uses the word 'spiritual' to talk of 'gifts', 'thoughts', 'words' and 'people',[101] it speaks of a divine interaction whereby the Holy Spirit enables us 'To do the right thing, at the right time, in the right way'. Being tuned in to the prompting of the Holy Spirit, we ready ourselves to receive an infinitesimal portion of God's all-knowing, and then prayerfully ask how the Father would have us use that knowledge to change the atmosphere in the room. Every individual or corporate meeting is a joint effort where the Holy Spirit is wanting to put us on like a coat so as to represent the interests of heaven on earth. You may be the oldest person in the room but age is not an issue when the executor of God's will is at work. Have a smile that lights up the room, greeting others in a way that tells them that they are appreciated, approved and accepted.

Every generation has its parents, church leaders and social workers who are working tirelessly to make headway in their chosen career. Crippled by self-doubt, overstretched and buried under a mountain of work, they are in desperate need of a helping hand. Lying beaten up beside the road of life they need to experience a Samaritan-type spirit that climbs down from their high horse, that offers a helping hand and the means for total restoration. To visually and vocally come alongside a fellow human so as to offer help is the true essence of the New Testament word 'encouragement'.

---

101. 1 Corinthians 12:1; 2:11-13; 3:1-3, NIV.

The Redman Factor

At the 1992 Summer Olympic Games in Barcelona, Spain, a qualifying heat of the men's 400 metres was about to take place. Having been forced to withdraw from the same event four years earlier through injury, Derek Redmond had missed out on a medal opportunity. Following numerous surgeries, the road to recovery had been hard and long. But now was not the time for looking back. Redmond needed to finish this race, as one of the four fastest qualifiers. This would give him a fighting chance to achieve his dream of an Olympic gold.

As Derek settled into the starting blocks, his father, Jim Redmond, who had been his constant training companion, was forced to spectate his son's race high up in the stands. With the sound of the starting gun still ricocheting around the stadium, Derek commenced an all-out bid to make it to the Olympic final. Quickly reaching his stride, the dream of a place in the 400 metre men's final was slowly becoming a reality. Running down the back straight he was gaining on the opposition, when 175 metres from the finishing line, disaster struck. Hearing a pop in his right hamstring Derek was literally stopped in his tracks. Pulling up lame, his running stride was quickly reduced to a hobble, before he collapsed to the ground in a pitiful heap.

Redman's dream of a gold medal was finished as the television commentator repeatedly yelled, 'Derek Redman is out of the race!' The TV cameras stayed fixed on the race as each of the remaining competitors made it the finishing line. Only when the race was over did the director decide to pan the cameras back to where a fallen runner was trying to pull himself up from the ground.

Having risen to his feet, Redman set off hobbling toward the finishing line, the mental and physical agony clearly visible on his tear-soaked face. Refusing to be sidelined by the race officials, Redman was determined to finish his race. As the crowd began to realise what this lame runner was attempting, they started to stand and cheer. When Redman later reflected on this moment, he would say, 'I wasn't doing it for me. Whether people thought I was an idiot or a hero, I wanted to finish the race.'[102]

As a lone figure limping in front of a crowd of 60,000 spectators, Derek had no idea that his father had already left his seat in the stands and was making his way to the edge of the track. Climbing the perimeter fence and brushing aside those track officials that tried to stop him, Jim somehow managed to make it to his son's side. Locked into a loving embrace, the son gained moral and physical support as together they made it to the finishing line.

The Redman narrative is not only a prophetic portrait of our loving heavenly Father – one who in Christ stepped down from the heavenly realm to embrace fallen humanity – mirrored within this tapestry of truth is a challenge to all third agers. For those guilty of grandstanding the affairs of heaven on earth, this is a wake-up call. Many sons and daughters of the King are struggling to complete their earthly assignment. In the light of this, seniors need to

---

102. Rick Weinberg, 'Derek and dad finish Olympic 4000 together', special to ESPN com, available from http//sports.espn.go.com/espn/espn25/story?page=moments/94 (accessed 15.7.25).

rise from our privileged positions and become spiritual alongsiders who offer their loving support and take their place in the ninth seat so as to steer and cheer those around them.

Question marks!

- Behaving like an old religious curmudgeon criticising a younger generation is not best practice for Christ followers, so how can we avoid such behaviour?

- Is it possible to cheer others when we ourselves do not feel cheerful?

- What does becoming an 'alongsider' mean in reality?

- Should we exhibit a 'Samaritan spirit' to those from a different background and belief system?

- How should we react to being sidelined from the affairs of heaven on earth?

6

Go For Yourself

With the exit doors firmly closed, passengers seated and the flight deck preparing for take-off, the voice of the captain could be heard saying: 'Good morning, ladies and gentlemen. On behalf of British Airways, I would like to take this opportunity of welcoming you to this flight to London, Heathrow. May we have your attention as the cabin crew point out the safety features on board this Airbus A320.'

Although frequent flyers have already stored their hand luggage, fastened their seat belts and mentally switched off, first-timers are hanging onto every word. Whether it's exit doors or emergency lighting, in case the unthinkable happens, they want their own well-rehearsed exit strategy.

As the cabin crew draw their briefing to a close, one crew member holds up an oxygen mask. Enacting a possible emergency scenario, they offer the following words of advice: 'In the case of a loss of cabin pressure, oxygen masks like these will fall automatically from the panel above your head. Pull the mask down sharply. Cover your mouth and nose. Secure with the elastic strap and breath normally.' For listeners and non-listeners alike, the following sentence could literally mean the difference between life and death.

'Only when you have secured your own mask, should you attend to children and other passengers.'

For those passengers unfortunate enough to experience an in-flight emergency, they have on average eighteen seconds to act on this advice. But imagine the dilemma facing a parent. Seeing their child gasping for air, they have a critical decision to make. Intuitively, they would sacrifice their own well-being for the sake of their children. But by refusing to apply their own oxygen mask first, they risk becoming incapacitated and therefore incapable of helping anyone. In this instance survival is an issue of self-care.

Is self-care selfish?

Having been raised by a self-sacrificing generation who secured our freedom through two world wars, many Baby Boomers struggle with the concept of self-care. Yet to dismiss the old adage 'looking after number one' as self-serving, self-seeking, narcissistic and egotistic, is problematic. For what happens when a toxic relationship, a controlling environment or abusive behaviour, leaves us breathless? To personally experience this 'loss of cabin pressure' that leaves us gasping for air will mean that we have a brief window of opportunity in which to prioritise our needs over those of others.

'But isn't Christianity founded on self-sacrifice, not self-serving?' I hear you say. And what of the words of Jesus, found in Mark's Gospel that says: 'If anyone would come after me, let him deny himself and take up his cross and follow me. For whoever would save his life will lose it, but whoever loses his life for my sake . . . will save it.'[103] But should any rhetoric regarding 'selflessness' drive us to the point of 'self-destruction'? In his book *Let Your Life Speak*, Parker Palmer writes:

> Self-care is never a selfish act – it is simply good stewardship of the only gift I have, the gift I was put on earth to offer others. Anytime we can listen to true self and give the care it requires, we do it not only for ourselves, but for the many others whose lives we touch.[104]

The human body is a work of art. Having created countless billions, God is still crafting unique one-of-a-kind masterpieces. But as with so many priceless artifacts, the human body is incredibly fragile. Using the phrase 'jars of clay',[105] the apostle Paul creates an analogy regarding the fragility of the human frame. Some translators prefer to use the imagery of an 'oyster shell' to speak of the priceless pearl of 'the knowledge of the glory of God',[106] contained within a brittle casing. But whether we speak of clay jars, bones or shells, the reality is the human body is easily broken and needs to be handled with care. But before getting ahead of ourselves, we should return to 'the elephant in the room', the one that advocates that 'Self-care is selfish'.

---

103. Mark 8:34-35, ESV.
104. Parker J. Palmer, *Let Your Life Speak: Listening for the Voice of Vocation* (San Francisco, CA: Jossey-Bass, 2000), p. 30.
105. 2 Corinthians 4:7.
106. 2 Corinthians 4:6.

Writing to those New Testament Christians living in Rome, the apostle Paul calls for 'sacrificial service'. However, he was speaking of becoming a 'living' rather than 'dying sacrifice'. To advocate the later would fly in the face of Christ's all-sufficient sacrificial death. *The Message* puts it this way: 'So here's what I want you to do, God helping you: Take your everyday, ordinary life – your sleeping, eating, going-to-work, and walking-around life – and place it before God as an offering.'[107]

On this issue the author Paul Swann in his book *Sustaining Leadership* should perhaps have the final word as he writes:

> To be self-destructive is not the same as being self-sacrificial. Of course, there is a cost to discipleship, but that cost is not supposed to be working yourself into ill-health, marital breakdown and dried-out spirituality. The sacrifice Paul calls for is a living sacrifice – in stark contrast to the slaughtered sacrifices of his time. Our sacrificial lives need to be sustainable enough for us to go on giving.[108]

If the antithesis of *self-care* is *self-neglect*, then any negligence that results in mental, physical or spiritual breakdown has to be seen as an anathema to those words spoken by a loving heavenly Father. For in those moments when people, objects or events cause a catastrophic 'loss of cabin pressure', we have to learn how to prioritise our needs above those of others. Sadly, something that Baby Boomers have, with the best of intentions, failed to observe.

107. Romans 12:1-2.
108. Paul Swann, *Sustaining Leadership* (Abingdon: Bible Reading Fellowship, 2018).

Couple of self-carers

The Old Testament narrative regarding Abram and Sarai is the story of two individuals called to a life of self-care. From the beginning of time, God's redemptive plan has always involved third agers. In Genesis 12 we observe the restorative nature of a loving heavenly Father, engaging two old-timers as ambassadors of heaven on earth.

From the *delights* of Genesis 1 and 2, through the *disaster* of chapters 3 and 4, to the *deluge* of chapters 6 to 8 and the *diversity* of Genesis 11, we come to the *defining moment* of Genesis 12.

Following the fiasco of Babel's Tower, where nations were formed, God began to birth his very own 'HOLY NATION',[109] a task he reserved for two retirees. Their call and commission, set within the framework of a covenantal promise, sets the scene for a present-day comeback in which seniors become re-engaged in the purposes of heaven on earth.

Revered by Christianity as the founding father of faith, Abram's epic journey from 'Ur of the Chaldeans to . . . Canaan' [110] is something of an allegory regarding living life in the last lane. As an outward-bound school majoring in faith, their pilgrimage is something of a roadmap for those performing in life's third act. Having decided to partner with the purpose of God, Abram and Sarai disassociated themselves from their extended family. Relatives who for more than half a century had 'settled'[111] for a life that fell far short God's ultimate intention. Those first tentative steps taken by these two geriatric go-getters were as crucial to

109. 1 Peter 2:9, NASB.
110. Genesis 11:31, ESV.
111. Genesis 11:31, NASB.

them as they are to us. Using intricate brush strokes, the biblical text paints a prophetic picture of third agers refusing to settle in 'a halfway house between ... a past that is over and a future yet to be'.[112]

In the original Hebrew text, the word translated 'Go' in Genesis 12:1 is repeated. Using the Hebrews words *lech l'cha*, translators give us a variation on a theme. The sentence, 'Go from your country and your kindred and your father's house' could equally be translated, 'Go, go *from* yourself', 'Go, go *for* yourself', or 'Go, go *find* yourself'.

- **'Go, go from yourself.'**

  In that his father's household had settled and spent more than a half-century in Haran, Abram and Sarai were no longer willing to be part of a community settling for second best.[113] In leaving his father's beloved hometown, Abram was disassociating himself *'from'* those people, places and philosophies that might distract or delay him from fulfilling the call of God on his life.

  Few realise the cost involved in Abram and Sarai's decision to depart. We might think in terms of a young person leaving their hometown to go to university. But for a so-called 'Boomerang Generation', there is, for the fortunate, the safety net of Mum and Dad to fall back on. In obedience to God's call, this ageing couple moved anyway from their extended family – a community which in terms

---

112. Richard L. Morgan, *The Bible Speaks to Third and Fourth Agers* (Abingdon: Bible Reading Fellowship, 2002), p. 11.
113. Genesis 11:31, NASB.

of an ancient civilisation was associated with long-term safety, support and security.

The call of God is costly. To separate ourselves from anything or anyone that might distract from the divine can prove socially expensive. While for some that separation may be momentary, for others it could be permanent. But to rid ourselves of negative associations, unhealthy relationships, toxic environments and controlling influences, is all part of what it means to 'go *from* yourself'. A moment of self-care fundamental to re-engaging in the purpose of heaven on earth.

- **'Go, go for yourself'**

Pivotal to the covenant promises found in the opening verses of Genesis 12 is a call to 'Go *for* yourself [for your own advantage] away from your country, from your relatives and your father's house, to the land that I will show you'.[114] They, like us, had to realise that 'nothing, absolutely nothing, is more powerful, more intimate, and more important than to listen to the call of God our Creator, and to realign yourself to the very purpose of life and the universe by following his call wherever your life leads'.[115]

The divine imperative associated with God's call to Abram and Sarai was this issue of looking after number one. To 'Go, go *for yourself*' is to look after yourself unapologetically; to not wait

---

114. Genesis 12:1-7, AMPC, emphasis mine.
115. Os Guinness, *The Call* (Nashville, TN: Thomas Nelson, 2018) , p. vii

for accreditation from others; to never settle for anything less than self-respect and self-love. Yet, for those Christians who have grown up under the umbrella of 'self-sacrifice', the idea of 'looking after number one' can prove incredibly challenging. Yet to become the best version of who God has intended us to be is somewhat reliant on this issue of 'self-care'. We maintain a motorised vehicle to achieve the maximum mileage, yet we so easily run ourselves into the ground. Without regular spiritual, mental, social and physical check-ups, we potentially run the risk of experiencing a breakdown that could potentially result in us becoming stranded on the hard shoulder of life's last lane.

Self-preservation is not selfish, it's strategic! Whether our preference is walking, running, fishing, drinking coffee, reading books or chatting to a close friend – we all need an environment in which we can become spiritually recharged, physically re-energised and mentally recalibrated. The time, resources and effort we are willing to invest into ourselves is reflective of the value we place on that most precious of resources – us. Like Abram and Sarai, to 'go *for* yourself' needs to become our modus operandi. A system by which our whole life operates.

- **'Go, go find yourself.'**

In his essay 'Self-Reliance' Ralph Waldo Emerson speaks of how life's greatest achievement is to be yourself in an environment that is constantly seeking to make you someone else.[116]

The journey to find and function as our true self is often difficult and demanding. Concerned that if people knew who we really are they would not accept, appreciate or approve of us, we feel compelled to camouflage the real us. If the real you is what you Think, Value, Love, Dislike, Desire, Believe in and are Committed to, etc., we all need a safe and secure environment in which we can function and flourish. When group dynamics overtly or covertly dictate that we become a facsimile of the most charismatic person in the room, we have to wake up to the reality that such is not the Christian community Christ died for.

As a unique, one-of-a-kind individual, it is only through our union and communion with Jesus Christ that we can progressively become the person God intended. In this way we can with the apostle Paul say, 'by the grace of God I am what I am'.[117] Authenticity requires honesty and honesty requires a godly community. Only within a safe environment will individuals begin to remove the masks of pretence without fear of rejection. For the journey to 'find yourself' is only possible through a personal relationship with Christ and those spiritual interactions found within a New Testament community.

---

116. Ralph Waldo Emerson, *Self-Reliance* (Garden City, NY: Dover Publications Inc., 2000).
117. 1 Corinthians 15:10, NASB.

With a sense of incompleteness, Abram and Sarai began their journey of self-discovery. As a childless couple, they lacked the wherewithal of their God-given inheritance. By working outside the divine parameters and taking matters into their own hands, they produced an Ishmael, when God had promised an Isaac. God alone would change their childless state. At the age of ninety-nine, Abram experienced a divine encounter that changed his name to 'father of a multitude'. At that critical moment Abraham and Sarah began to experience the reality of their reason for being. For us to find and fulfil our ageless identity in Christ requires a journey of faith.

Metronome moments

When pastor, author and speaker John Ortberg asked his mentor Dallas Willard, 'What do I need to do to become the me I want to be?' His answer, that would ultimately form the basis of Ortberg's book, *The Me I Want to Be* was, 'You must ruthlessly eliminate hurry from your life.'[118] What Willard was referring to was the need to find time to be in tune with the purpose of God.

---

118. John Mark Comer, *The Ruthless Elimination of Hurry*, (London: Hodder & Stoughton, 2019), p. 18.

Anyone with a shred of musical skill could tell that I was murdering Ludwig van Beethoven's first movement of his *Moonlight Sonata*. To quote a famous English comedian Eric Morecambe, 'I was playing all the right notes, but maybe not in the right order!' Being out of time with what the original creator intended this was what my old musical teacher called a 'Metronome Moment'. Sitting silently on top of the upright grand piano, the wooden cased metronome was a practical clockwork instrument that produce a steady audible beat. A machine that helps would-be musicians to restore their rhythm to what the original composer had in mind.

Jesus put it this way:

Are you tired? Worn out? Burned out on religion? Come to me. Get away with me and you'll recover your life. I'll show you how to take a real rest. Walk with me and work with me – watch how I do it. Learn the unforced rhythms of grace. I won't lay anything heavy or ill-fitting on you. Keep company with me and you'll learn to live freely and lightly.[119]

Taking time out in order to restore those 'rhythms of grace' is to take Willard's advice and 'ruthlessly eliminate hurry from your life.'

When what was initially fun becomes frightening, we need to stop. When ministry life becomes a manic merry-go-round that leaves us nauseated and suffering from spiritual vertigo, we need to press the pause button! When life becomes an emotional roller-coaster of relentless highs and lows, we need to step away so as to restore those godly rhythms of grace. For 'me time' is the divine imperative to being human. A moment in which we disassociate ourselves *from* those distractive forces and apply the oxygen mask of God's grace *for* ourselves and begin to *find* the best version of ourselves.

Hold the front page

When the Harvard Business School, in Boston, Massachusetts, USA, undertook a four-year survey into retirees, they had

---

119. Matthew 11:28-30, *MSG*.

little idea as to what they would discover. For while social media portrays retirement as silver-haired couples walking hand-in-hand along some far-flung sandy beach, the reality is often quite different. For many, giving up their career is not the perfect picture they imagined. After the initial euphoria of leaving full-time employment, many are left feeling undervalued and under-utilised.

Answering the question, 'How would you describe yourself?' some of those taking part in the Harvard study responded: 'I'm a retired librarian' or 'I'm a retired educator' or 'I'm a retired research chemist'. Wondering why retirees would insist on attaching a former profession to their response, Professor Teresa Amabile explained:

> Some will deny being retired ... they will say what their profession is even though they're not working in that profession any more. We asked them why they do this and they say it's because they don't want to be seen as someone who is out to pasture. One person said 'I don't want to be seen as yesterday's news I want to be the news right now.'[120]

While appreciating the group's honesty, one has to wonder if society is wilfully editing an older generation out of the human narrative. Has a youth-obsessed culture become complicit in burying the so-called longevity revolution at the bottom of page seven? If true, this would be tragic.

But hold the front page!

120. Ian Rose, 'Why we lie about being retired', 20 August 2019, www.bbc.co.uk > news > business-48882195 (accessed 25.7.25).

What if seniors were to push back? Seeing themselves as principal characters in today's narrative, they refused to be marginalised? Like Abram and Sarai, they could take steps to re-engage themselves in the affairs of heaven on earth. Believing that life in the last lane is more about integration than isolation, third agers could embrace a holy dissatisfaction regarding the present state of affairs and begin to vocalise their concerns.

The First Arab Spring was a mass popular uprising of people with unfulfilled aspirations. In the early 2010s individuals took to the streets to protest against the autocratic rulers of Middle Eastern countries. These public demonstrations quickly spread across much of the Arab world. While facing fierce opposition, their goal was to challenge entrenched ideologies that were stifling people's hopes and aspirations.

As long as church leaders equate age with ability, they run the risk of fuelling a silver riot. To lead with a declinist view of age and the ageing process is to risk a popular uprising of revolutionary retirees. Not that an army of placard-waving grey-haired protestors are about to picket church buildings. But rather than suffer in silence, maybe it's time for those old warhorses tired of being hitched to an ageist agenda to respectfully air their grievances; to speak out against those entrenched ideologies and their unfulfilled aspirations regarding life in the last lane.

If necessary, God will shake the shakeable, in order to establish his unshakable kingdom.[121] Faced with a youth-obsessed Christianity in which retirees are left feeling

---

121. Hebrews 12:27.

undervalued and under-utilised, nothing short of a shift in the tectonic plates of present thinking will suffice. Increasingly, the scene is being set for a generational comeback in which seniors will no longer discount themselves but occupy those vacancies in the areas of expertise, experience, wisdom and networking ability for which they are well-qualified.

Comeback

On Tuesday afternoon 26 February 2008, every Starbucks across North America closed its doors to retrain its baristas. A simple note was posted on the door of each store that read: 'We're taking time to perfect our Espresso. Great expresso requires practice. That's why we're dedicating ourselves to honing our craft.'[122]

Having stepped down from the position of CEO, the Starbucks founder, Howard Schultz, was being forced to make a managerial comeback. With an all-consuming passion for the company, he could see that Starbucks was beginning to lose its way. From Schultz's perspective, the original *vision* was being lost through a change of *vehicle*. In what is often referred to as the episode of the 'Burnt Cheese Sandwich', on entering one particular Starbucks store, instead of being greeted by the sweet aroma of roasted coffee beans, Schultz was confronted with the smell of burnt cheese sandwiches. During his absence, the company had diversified into offering customers a cooked

---

122. Howard Schultz, with Joanne Gordan, *Onward: How Starbucks Fought for Its Life without Losing Its Soul* (Bognor Regis: John Wiley & Sons, 2011).

breakfast. Incensed by the departure from Starbucks' original vision and values, Howard Schultz made the comeback of all comebacks.

Howard Schultz, like many founders, has made managerial changes he lived to regret. While the intention to make way for the new and the young was honourable, a poorly executed succession plan has often proven disastrous. With no one to guide them, orphaned leaders easily became lost in an uncharted managerial maze. When placed under new management, secular and spiritual organisations can experience a season in which the novice leaders break ties with the past. Looking for the means to attract new 'customers', they implement radical changes to the menu. Without any thought of the vision and values of the founding fathers, changes are implemented that inevitably result in an unpleasant aroma.

Howard Schultz did not merely love Starbucks, he lived it. As lovers of the Church, many third agers are ready and waiting to return to frontline activity. With a pungent smell of performance-orientated Christian gatherings, the return of an older generation could create that sweet aroma of a gospel partnership that the apostle Paul spoke of.[123] Whether their comeback is as counsellors, coaches, cheerleaders or critical friends, their return could bring about a spiritual renaissance in terms of community life as God intended.

To make the necessary comeback, third agers will need to:

---

123. Philippians 4:14-23.

- Lose the air of superiority;

- Learn the dynamics of second-chair leadership;

- Listen to those younger and less experienced individuals now in positions of authority;

- Lead from a place of security and daily draw on the oxygen of God's amazing grace;

- Latch onto the 'necessary no' and the 'essential yes'.

Question marks!

- Are you presently facing 'an oxygen mask moment' in which people, objects and events are sucking the air out of the room? Is so, how can you make self-care a priority?

- Rather than yesterday's news, how in a positive way can retirees become tomorrow's headlines?

- Do the people you know, know the real you?

- If becoming the best version of ourselves requires self-investment, how are you planning to invest?

7

Don't Stuff the Dead Dog!

When the American actor Alan Alda entitled his memoir *Never Have Your Dog Stuffed*, not only did he manage to publish a fascinating story, he gave the world a parable about the reality of progressive change.

With a wry sense of humour, this Emmy and Golden Globe winner related a life lesson taken from his childhood. Based on the tragic, but somewhat humorous, tale surrounding the death of his pet dog Rhapsody, Alda painted a picture of how we handle the inevitable seasons of change. Inseparable in life, Alan was inconsolable over the loss of his childhood companion.

Trying to comfort the young lad, Alan's father made a somewhat rash promise: 'Rhapsody will return.'

Unknown to the heartbroken boy, his dad had asked a local taxidermist to work his magic on the canine. Unfortunately, having never seen the animal alive, his efforts to resurrect Rhapsody and return him to some form of normality resulted in creating something woefully out of tune with reality. The reality is that you can never recognise the fake unless you've experienced the genuine. On Rhapsody's return, it soon became clear that in seeking to preserve the past, the taxidermist had inadvertently created a present-day monster. Explaining Rhapsody's reunion Alan Alda wrote:

> We pulled off the brown butcher's paper he was wrapped in and looked at him. The dog had a totally unrecognisable expression on his face. He looked as if he'd seen something loathsome that needed to be shredded . . . Losing the dog wasn't as bad as getting him back.[124]

Visitors to the family home now had to be forewarned that the dog in the living room wasn't real. The canine's poise convinced onlookers that this ferocious-looking animal was in desperate need of human flesh. Even when demoted to the porch, deliverymen would do anything to avoid the house.

Monuments out of moments

The moral of the story is 'that stuffing your dog is . . . what happens when you hold on to any living moment longer than it wants you to'.[125] Although he had been a much-loved family pet, Rhapsody's reincarnation was a constant reminder that things would never be the way they were. While his father's motives were good, in attempting to hang onto the past he created a lifeless form.

---

124. Alan Alda, *Never Have Your Dog Stuffed* (London: Arrow Books, Kindle, 2007), location 348-385.
125. Alda, *Never Have Your Dog Stuffed*, location 385.

As glorious a moment in time might be, the danger is that we pitch our tent around it and create a movement that eventually becomes a monument. In the midst of the brilliance of Christ's transfiguration, Peter's impetuous response was to build something, to put up a tent so as to camp around that particular revelatory moment in time.[126] History teaches us that Christianity has a propensity to camp around a particular aspect of God's ongoing revelatory truth. Pioneers become settlers who create movements entrenched in manmade traditions. When God's people are unwilling to move on, they inadvertently taxidermy divine truth in a lifeless form. Peter had forgotten that God in Christ was no longer confined to a tabernacle or temple; the Word had become flesh and had 'moved into the neighborhood'.[127] When referring back to this incident, John, with a different perspective from Peter, wrote: 'We proclaim to you what we have seen and heard, so that you also may have fellowship with us.'[128]

Old dogs and new tricks

In seeking to preserve the past, we potentially miss out on God's preferred future. Putting new wine into old wineskins is a metaphor illustrating this very mindset.[129] God's revelatory truth is powerful and cannot be contained in old, rigid structures and set ways of thinking. Constant

---

126. Matthew 17:1-9, NIV.
127. John 1:14, *MSG*.
128. 1 John 1:3, NIV.
129. Matthew 9:17; Mark 2:22; Luke 5:37-39.

change is here to stay and we need to learn how to preserve God's changeless Word in an ever-changing world.

While resistance to change is futile, some third agers feel as if they are being dragged kicking and screaming into the twenty-first century – technophobes for whom surfing the World Wide Web is as scary as literally riding the waves off the North Shore, Oahu, Hawaii. In those moments when honesty reigns, many seniors would confess to feeling like time-travellers, transported to another planet. Frozen in time, they have become Gutenberg people in a Google world.[130] People who in true Luddite fashion would much rather hold onto the past than accept God-ordained change. Yet no matter the teacher or the subject, every day is a classroom experience from which we should never play truant. If we are to graduate from God's finishing school, every day has to become a learning opportunity.

When seniors adopt an 'Old Dog New Tricks' mindset and become inflexible in their beliefs and behaviour, they are unlikely to learn anything new. Thankfully, the learning environment in the Jewish temple in Jesus' day was different. For here we find some older teachers in Jerusalem listened to and learned from a twelve-year-old Jewish boy.[131] On the cusp of adulthood, Jesus conversed with those older Jewish scholars. In so doing, they exemplified a key characteristic by which inter-generational churches will be characterised. An ageless community in which people from different generations genuinely interact with each other. However, within Western civilisation a malfunctioning methodology has created something of a learning dilemma.

---

130. Referring to mid-fifteenth century Gutenberg press.
131. Luke 2:41-52.

Mention the phrase 'to learn' and most Westerners think of classes, courses or curriculum. A frame of reference rooted in a Greek, rather than Hebrew (biblical) model of learning.

So much of modern education is built around academic achievement, the ability to retain information, rather experiencing transformative truth. When Jesus taught, 'The people were amazed [marveled] and said, 'This man has never studied in school. How did he learn so much?'[132] Such supernatural schooling was mirrored in his disciples who were described as 'unlearned and untrained in the schools [common men with no educational advantages], they marveled; and they recognized that they had been with Jesus'.[133]

Influenced by people like Socrates, Plato and Aristotle, Western methodology has created a classroom culture. Modern education has created a student/teacher environment that is systematic, analytical, formal and organised, whereas the Hebrew (biblical) model was more relational than transactional in style. For here truth is *caught* and not just *taught.*

Having spent their early years in the synagogue memorising biblical text, 'those who were apprenticed to [Jesus]'[134] were taken on a three-year mentorship journey. This group of teachable teenagers walked, talked and observed 24/7 the ways of Rabbi Jesus. Parenting these sons of the kingdom, Jesus followed a Mosaic parenting model. He would, 'Talk about [God's commandments] wherever [they were], sitting at home or walking in the street; talk

---

132. John 7:15, EXB.
133. Acts 4:13, AMPC.
134. Matthew 5:1, *MSG.*

about them from the time [they got] up in the morning to when you fall into bed at night.'[135] Jesus' wholistic teaching style was both relational and situational. The whole of life became a learning process and their daily environment, an interactive classroom. This was situational learning at its best. Whether a fig tree, farmer or a funeral cortège, Jesus made every day a learning opportunity.

Refusing to accept change, and remaining entrenched in an old mindset, is symptomatic of someone trying to taxidermy truth. By insisting on 'new things' fitting into 'old ways,' we enlist ourselves in the ranks of the great unlearned. And although an unteachable spirit is no respecter of age it will over time display some, if not all of, of the following characteristics:

- Stagnation or shrinkage in terms of spiritual growth;
- Failure to maximise personal potential;
- Relying on past revelation;
- Demonstrate a fixed mindset and a know-it-all-attitude;
- Stale communication;
- Lacking curiosity, wonderment, self-awareness and motivation;
- Hating feedback and having to be right all the time.

Super seniors

Humanity has always dreamed of living forever. Since the start of the twentieth century, in the United States of

---

135. Deuteronomy 6:7, *MSG*.

America, life expectancy has increased by thirty years from forty-nine in 1900 to almost seventy-nine today – with more and more people living into their mid-eighties upwards. For those known as the 'Oldest Old',[136] studies show that these super seniors follow a regime that aligns itself with the philosophy of Albert Einstein that says: 'Once you stop learning, you start dying.'

Dr Manfred Steiner received a doctorate in physics at the age of eighty-nine. Having completed a thirty-plus-year career in medicine, Steiner's latest degree was one step nearer to realising his childhood dream of becoming a physicist. Speaking of this new phenomena, Alex Zhavoronkov wrote:

> More than ever, we are seeing other examples of seniors in their eighties and beyond continuing to enrich the world with their achievement instead of settling into the decrepit old age far too many people pessimistically see in their own future.[137]

Yuichiro Miura reached the summit of Mount Everest at the age of eighty. What was previously seen as 'off limits' for seniors is no longer so. Education is no longer the preserve of the young. More and more elderly people are going back to college and earning degrees. Nola Ochs, a Kansas woman, earned her Bachelor's degree at ninety-five and then went on to earn a Master's degree at the age of ninety-eight – even moving into the campus dorms. 'She

136. *Improving later life. Understanding the oldest old,* Michelle Mitchell, www.ageuk. org.uk (accessed 25.7.25).
137. Alex Zhavoronkow, PhD, '5 Ways To Stay Younger And More Creative As You Get Older', www.forbes.com (accessed 11.3.22).

hopes to encourage people to keep on learning and tells her grandchildren, "If grandmother can do it, you can".[138] Within my own circle of friends there are those who in their seventies and eighties are still actively involved in church leadership, counselling, songwriting, evangelism, leading worship, authoring books, volunteering in hospital and refusing to leave the mission field.

What makes these super seniors so vibrant and active in their advancing years is their attitude towards lifelong learning. With a spring in their step, every day is a classroom in which they adopt the role of both student and teacher. While the student assumes a learning posture, the teacher within wants to share the lessons learned, and the mistakes made over a lifetime, with anyone willing to listen.

Old age is not a disqualifier. When unceremoniously removed from any kind of interactive classroom, those previously seen as essential participants are progressively being shut out. Feeling surplus to requirements, many people in the second half of life are being systematically ignored, isolated and treated as invisible. Sidelined from the field of play, while some seniors are sticking around hoping against hope to be included in team selection, others are making a pre-emptive strike by excusing themselves from the game altogether. Wrongly believing they have nothing worthwhile to contribute, they have made themselves unavailable for selection. In so doing, old age is fast becoming a spectator sport of Olympic proportion. Such behaviour portrays a gross misunderstanding of God's

---

138. Welbi.co/blog/10-amazing=accomplishments-by-seniors, 13 September 2017, accessed date unknown.

purpose for those of advancing years. To grandstand any season of life is to misunderstand the true meaning of childhood, adulthood or elderhood. When our latter years degenerate into a waiting-room experience in which we sit back and wait for the inevitable, life becomes a self-fulfilling prophecy.

To live with a lapsed sense of purpose is not the grand finale a loving heavenly Father has scripted for any of us. For the curtain to fall on a life well lived, our final act should be played out in such a way as to bring a standing ovation from heaven's great 'cloud of witnesses'.[139] To regret the past, be indifferent to the present and nervously awaiting the future is to ignore the divine possibility that says, 'If we're not dead, then God's not done.'

Even when becoming understudies to those who have taken on those roles and responsibility we once occupied, super seniors not only stand ready to cheer their protégés on, but if necessary, lovingly prompt them when they stumble over their words. For as seniors move on to new spheres of active service, the success of others becomes their success.

Speaking of life as a daily learning experience, Alvin Toffler, the futurist, author and philosopher, warns that:

The illiterate of the 21st century will not be those who cannot read and write, but those who cannot learn, unlearn, and relearn.[140]

---

139. Hebrews 12:1.
140. John Hennessy, *Embracing the Need to 'Learn and Relearn'*, Stanford Magazine, January/February 2002, quoting Alvin Toffler.

Unlearning has become the new learning, and no one should underestimate the disruptive power of old thinking. A paradigm shift can take an excruciating amount of time and require an extreme amount of effort. The mental journey from *'thinking old and doing old'*, via *'thinking new and doing old'*, to the ultimate destination of *'thinking new and doing new'*, is long and arduous. But when seniors become entrenched in old methodology, they risk being dismissed as spiritual dinosaurs.

Pivotal people

Being well into his nineties, the biblical Daniel, of lions' den fame, lived in a constant state of readiness to pivot the purpose of heaven on earth. Having stepped aside from serving in the king's court, when an opportunity came knocking, Daniel was ready to interpret God's word to a confused generation.[141]

History is a hinge on which the future swings – a pivotal moment in which one generation speaks into the next. Being a pivotal prophet, John the Baptist was 'The voice of one crying in the wilderness'.[142] Standing on a tipping-point in time, John became a pivotal person between the old and new – he bridged humanity's past with God's preferred future. Calling out a spirit of religiosity, his preferred diet, dress code and dwelling place exemplified a life totally dependent on God. Like the camel-coated, locust-eating wilderness-dweller, twenty-first-century Christianity stands

---

141. Daniel 5.
142. Matthew 3:3, ESV.

at a pivotal point in time. Society doesn't need archaic religious systems or critical echoes from the past, it needs anointed voices to lovingly speak of God's never-changing Word, into an ever-changing world.

As difficult and different the ageing process is, third agers are called to guide the next generation in the ways of the Kingdom. To engage in a dynamic mentoring relationship that should have been exemplified between an ageing priest called Eli, and his young protégé, Samuel. In adopting an unteachable attitude, Eli illustrates the need to be observant, listen and adopt a learning lifestyle that enables us to disciple others, because . . .

We taxidermy God's truth when we stop . . .

- **Looking**

    Sight and perception are different. In the eighth chapter of Mark's Gospel a formerly blind man, for whom Jesus had prayed for healing, was asked if he could see. His response was, 'I see men as trees'.[143] He had sight, but lacked perception.

    The degenerative state of Eli's eyesight seemed to parallel his loss of spiritual perception. When Hannah earnestly prayed for a child in the temple, Eli perceived her to be 'a drunken woman'.[144] From a state of growing 'dim' (KJV) to a point at which his eyes were 'fixed' (NASB) or 'set' (ESV) in their sockets, Eli's eyesight was progressively worsening.

---

143. Mark 8:24, KJV.
144. 1 Samuel 1:13, ESV.

Having lost his peripheral vision, this ninety-eight-year-old priest became too blinkered to see what was tragically unfolding around him. Unlike Daniel, Eli was unable to interpret God's now word to the next generation.[145]

A classic scene in the movie *Patch Adams* (1998) starring Robin Williams is when Adams, struggling with suicidal thoughts, voluntarily admits himself into a mental institution. While wandering around the hospital, he meets a fellow inmate called Arthur Mendelson (Harold Gould). A wealthy mathematician, it's Mendelson who first gives 'Patch' his nickname. Through this meeting of minds, Adams gains a fresh outlook on life.

Entering Mendelson's room, Patch is desperate to find the answer to a simple equation Mendelson had posed. Holding up four fingers, Mendelson asks Patch how many digits he can see. When Patch says 'four' Mendelson reprimands him. 'If you focus on the problem, you can't see the solution. Never focus on the problem. . . . Look beyond the fingers . . . See what no one else sees. See what everyone else chooses not to see out of fear, of conformity and laziness. See the whole world view anew each day.'[146] Looking beyond the immediate, Patch begins to see the blurry form of eight fingers.

Any spiritual stigmatism that creates either blurred or blinkered vision will blindside third agers from interpreting the ongoing purposes of God to the next

145. 1 Samuel 4:12-18.
146. *Patch Adams*, Universal Studios, 1998.

generation. Pivotal people are prophetic people, individuals who see beyond the immediate into God's ultimate. Only seeing the obvious will make us oblivious to God's ultimate.

Young Samuel needed an older Eli to help him discern the voice of God – to think beyond the natural into the supernatural realm. But as someone whose spiritual, social and physical disciplines were lacking, Eli's mentoring skills were at an all-time low.

There is a Samuel generation presently volunteering in God's house who desperately need an older generation to wake up and smell the coffee! Society needs men and women, like the ageing Moses, who although '120 years old when he died. His eye was undimmed, and his vigour unabated'.[147] Samuels need seniors who are prophetically able to see what God is seeing and say what God is saying. Believer priests, who take their younger counterparts by the hand and lead them in the ways of God.

We taxidermy God's truth when we stop . . .

- **Listening**

Having spent her early life in Africa, Tina's family have a plethora of unforgettable stories. My personal favourite concerns Uncle Dai and the crocodile. Dai was a family friend, serving with Tina's father in the Royal Air Force in Kenya. As a dedicated angler,

---

147. Deuteronomy 34:7, ESV.

Dai would spend his downtime fishing in the local river. On this particular occasion Tina and her older sister happened to be crossing a bridge when they saw Uncle Dai fishing. Being some distance away, Tina had to shout to get Dai's attention. So, with no malice intended, she innocently shouted, 'Uncle Dai, are there any crocodiles in this river?' However, what Dai actually heard was, 'Uncle Dai, is that a crocodile in the river?' Blissfully minding his own business, smoking his pipe and enjoying a quiet moment of meditation, his serenity was shattered. Hearing the word, *'Crocodile'* Dai panicked. Scrabbling for safety from a supposed vicious predator, he inadvertently lost his balance and ended up in the river. With the loss of dignity along with his favourite smoking pipe, this tale of woe has down the years become a much-embellished family favourite.

Filtered or partial hearing can prove problematic. Jesus' parable of the sower is in some translations peppered with the phrase, 'He who has ears to hear, let him hear.'[148] Jesus wanted those apprenticed to him to 'take care how [they] listen'.[149] However, from their subsequent sailing disaster, it's clear they were poor listeners and hence slow learners. Even though staying after class to ask for further clarification regarding the parable, the disciples failed to activate faith in the spoken word. Such is evidenced by the fact that Jesus said, 'Let *us*' (plural) 'go over to the

---

148.   Luke 8:8, ESV.
149.   Luke 8:18, NASB.

other side'.[150] Having faith in the spoken word should have enabled the disciples to stand on the word and rebuke the wind and waves working in direct contradiction to God's declared will! Such prophetic action was within the disciples' mandate, but becoming overwhelmed with their surroundings, they missed an opportunity to speak a word of faith into their situation.

Looking and listening are fundamental principles to a disciple's learning lifestyle. These key factors were somewhat lacking in the interplay between an ageing Eli and his young protégé. Making a dramatic appearance onto the stage of Scripture, the initial performance of a twelve-year-old Samuel was a lesson in listening. While an ageing Eli lacked *discipline*, young Samuel, through no fault of his own, lacked *discernment*.

Samuel was a class act and would in time become the greatest of the Old Testament prophets. He served a nation that was falling apart at the seams. His willingness to hone his hearing skills and serve the purpose of God in obscurity would be the prelude to an extraordinary prophetic ministry.

At a time when the 'word from the LORD was rare . . . [and] visions . . . infrequent',[151] and surrounded by non-listeners, Samuel was about to lead a vanguard of prophetic listeners. While an elderly Eli was religiously going through the motions, Samuel needed to discern the difference between 'natural

---

150. Luke 8:22, NIV, emphasis mine.
151. 1 Samuel 3:1, NASB.

noise' and God's 'supernatural voice'. Yet it took three occasions of disturbed sleep for Eli to finally wake up to the reality that God was calling.

Amidst the cacophony of sound surrounding today's younger generation, third agers cannot afford to go through the motions of church-as-usual. To be spiritually asleep on our watch is unacceptable. There are faithful Samuels serving in God's house who need seniors to wake up to their God-given assignment and school the next generation.

We taxidermy God's truth when we stop . . .

- **Learning**

American business magnate Bill Gates is said to enrich his life by taking short retreats along with twenty-plus books to read. Why does a multi-billionaire at the pinnacle of his career want to rest and read widely? The answer is found in the fact that all great leaders are avid readers.[152] The vast amount of knowledge, expertise and experience our lives have already accrued should never stop us from adopting an attitude of continuous improvement through a learning lifestyle. Life is a university which we graduate when our time on earth is done.

Regurgitating stories everyone in the room has heard before is so often characteristic of someone who has checked out of class. Every day is a learning

---

152. www.lollydaskal.com/leadership/how-the-best-leaders-invest-in-themselves/ (accessed 15.7.25).

experience. To be present in the moment is to look, listen and learn fresh spiritual revelation. Speaking yesterday's language into today's world is to live with an old paradigm. By refusing to opt out of class and enrolling in a lifelong learning programme, we will become those seen as the super seniors, pivotal people that twenty-first-century Christianity so desperately needs.

Bigger jackets

Despite a defunct priesthood, young Samuel grew physically and spiritually. As if to highlight his physical development, his mother's annual visit would include an item of clothing. 'Samuel was ministering before the LORD, a boy clothed with a linen ephod. And his mother used to make for him a *little robe* and take it to him each year when she went up with her husband to offer the yearly sacrifice.'[153] So as to accommodate Samuel's physical growth, Hannah's yearly gift would

---

153. 1 Samuel 2:18-19, ESV, emphasis mine.

need to be a 'bigger jacket'. Yet, 'Little Samuel was growing in two ways – he was getting taller, and he was becoming everyone's favorite (and he was a favorite of the Lord's, too!).'[154]

While Samuel was growing physically, he was also developing socially and spiritually. From a solitary voice in the confines of the tabernacle, to becoming Israel's greatest prophet, Samuel's learning lifestyle would in time increase his sphere of influence.

Typically, old people physically shrink with age. Yet what is unavoidable in the natural should not be mirrored in the spiritual. For like the biblical Christ, we should be continually 'increasing in wisdom and stature, and in favor with God and people'.[155] To grow tall in the knowledge of who we are in Christ; to mature through a regular diet of revelatory truth; to develop a deeper relationship with a loving heavenly Father; to put away childish behaviour; to influence those around us with the gospel of the kingdom – is to increase in our spiritual stature.

Just as a creature sheds its skin to accommodate fresh growth, so treating every day as a learning experience will cause us to discard old thinking so as to accommodate a bigger version of the person God intends us to be. To break out of the mental cocoon that encapsulated a former way of life requires a metamorphosis of the mind. 'The renewing of the mind, so that you may prove [in practice] what the will of God is [for your life].'[156]

---

154.   1 Samuel 2:26, TLB, compare 3:19; Luke 2:40-52, NASB.
155.   Luke 2:52, NASB.
156.   Romans 12:2, paraphrased.

When instigating the Montgomery bus boycott as part of the social protest against racial segregation in the United States, Rosa Parks learned to shed the skin of racial inequality. She had determined that 'I will no longer act on the outside in a way that contradicts the truth I hold deeply on the inside. I will no longer act as if I were less than the whole person I know myself inwardly to be'.[157] In so doing she refused to taxidermy the truth and 'hold on to any living moment longer than it wants you to'.[158]

157. Rebekah Lyons, *You are Free Be Who You Already Are* (Grand Rapids, MI: Zondervan, 2017), p. 59.
158. Alda, *Never Have Your Dog Stuffed*, location 385.

147

Question marks!

- Is there anything that we are trying to revive that we should be letting go?

- Has today been a learning experience? If so what have you learned, unlearned or re-learned?

- What aspects of the 'old me' am I seeking to let go of in order to accommodate the 'new me' in Christ?

- What does the 'bigger jacket principle' say to you?

8

How Time Flies

Not far from the towering beauty of St Peter's Basilica in Rome lies a small and somewhat insignificant church building called Santa Maria della Concezione dei Cappuccini. For those visitors willing to leave the beauty of its single nave and descend into its dim, dusty basement crypt, a grim memorial to Time awaits.

In the eighteenth century, a secretive sect of men reinterred the remains of 4,000 of their deceased brothers. These were the same Capuchin monks who, with their distinct pointed hats, gave their name to coffee topped with foam – cappuccino. The Capuchin Crypt is lined with numerous human skeletal remains, some still dressed in their monk's habits. The walls and ceiling are decorated in such a way as to create an assortment of macabre works of art. Looking more like a Hollywood film set for the latest horror movie, few visitors linger long enough to appreciate their elaborate ornamental designs. Most tend to move quickly on to view the splendid works of art in the nearby Vatican Museums.

By creating this stark reminder to the fleeting nature of life, those Capuchin monks wanted visitors to stop and consider their own mortality, death and the divine. The reality of which is encapsulated in a Latin text, which translated reads:

What you are now, we used to be;
What we are now, you will be.[159]

Fifteen simple words that ask visitors to think of their *past* and *future*, while still living in the *present*. For what seemed endless as a child becomes increasingly limited as an adult. As with each passing moment the psalmist's prayer becomes more imperative, 'Teach us [Lord] to number our days'.[160] Time, like health, is easily taken for granted; that is, until either begins to fade.

Time tutors

The 20 January 1970 is a moment in time indelibly etched on my memory. As a twenty-four-year-old Bible college student called out of class to take an urgent telephone call, I had little idea as to the catastrophic events about to unfurl. Sensing something was wrong, I quickly ascertained that the person calling me was my church minister. His voice was full of hesitancy as he slowly began to relate the devastating news. That afternoon on her way to minister at a church gathering, my mother had suffered a fatal heart attack.

Sending shockwaves throughout the whole family, we struggled to grasp the reality of how our energetic fifty-

159. Philip Zimbardo, *The Time Paradox: Using the New Psychology of Time to Your Advantage'* (London: Rider, 2010).
160. Psalm 90:10-12, ESV.

seven-year-old mother could have been taken from us so soon and so suddenly. As the news of her passing started to sink in, we began to realise that we would never again hear those dulcet tones singing her favourite hymns. Her words of wisdom and contagious laughter would no longer echo around the family home. And never again would we be greeted with her warm, motherly embrace.

As a follower of Jesus, our mother walked in the footsteps of the great short-lived. And while shocking for us, the possibility of a short life was something she had already come to terms with. Taking nothing for granted, every day was a gift. Time was a priceless commodity and she could ill-afford to waste a moment. Daily busying herself in some form of family, church or business activity, as long as she had breath to breathe, she would live each day sensing the brevity of life.

The phrase 'Time is of the essence' is a legal term used in British Contractual Agreements. It speaks of two parties agreeing that certain actions must be taken within a set timeframe and is used to emphasise how humanitarian relief is time-sensitive for a country ravaged by war. Within a limited window of opportunity, certain actions must be undertaken that could mean the difference between life and death. Living each day with a divine destiny consciousness, our mother saw life as a fleeting moment – a set timespan predetermined in the heart of a loving heavenly Father. Her life acknowledged the biblical words of Job: '[Lord] You have decided the length of our lives. You know how many months we will live, and we are not given a minute longer.'[161]

---

161. Job 14:5, NLT.

I stand on the shoulders of Winifred May Spicer, a godly woman who became my time teacher. In the margins of her well-worn King James Bible was a handwritten note that was both simple yet profound. Although the language is somewhat archaic, the biblical verse from the book of James reads: 'Whereas ye know not what shall be on the morrow. For what is your life? It is even a vapour, that appeareth for a little time, and then vanisheth away.'[162] It was alongside this verse that our mother had added the marginal note, 'Little Time!'

This measurement of time motivated her to make the most of each passing moment. Time tutors are those irreplaceable individuals who speak into our lives about the use and abuse of time. Friends and family members who will graduate from the university of life, having majored in the subject of time. Yet, no matter how valid their legacy, they pale into insignificance when considering the life and teachings of the Lord Jesus Christ.

Time redeemers

Stepping out of eternity into a time/space continuum, Jesus modelled time management to perfection. No one should make light of his achievement. Becoming fully human, the incarnate Christ experienced all the stress and strain we experience. There is therefore no one more suited to teach us how to value, manage and redeem time, like the biblical Jesus. Or as Tim Keller puts it, 'Besides being vulnerable,

---

162. James 4:14, KJV.

subject to injury and death, [Jesus] had the limitations of being confined to one place in time and space.'[163]

In his book *Redeeming Your Time,* Jordan Raynor gives us a splendid overview of the life of Christ in terms of time. He writes:

> The Gospels do show [Jesus] prioritizing where he spent his time (see Mark 1:38), dealing with distractions at work (see Matthew 12:46-50), fighting for silence (see 14:13), and seeking to be busy without being hurried (see Mark 11:11). In other words, the Gospels show Jesus facing many of the same challenges we face today as we seek to steward our time. And because he was infallible God, we can assume that Jesus managed his time perfectly, providing us with the ideal model to follow.[164]

What we value we appreciate, and what we appreciate we give our attention to.

Locking ourselves into another non-stop Netflix series or becoming addicted to social media quickly depreciates the currency of time. When the kingdom of God takes a backseat to our busy lifestyle, we are likely to fall foul of wasting time on unproductive pursuits. That is why the apostle Paul urges us not to 'waste [our] time on useless work, mere busywork', what he calls 'the barren pursuits of darkness'.[165]

---

163. Timothy Keller, *Encounters with Jesus: Unexpected Answers to Life's Biggest Questions* (New York: Penguin Books, 2013), p. 175.
164. Jordan Raynor, *Redeeming Your Time* (London: Penguin Random House, 2021), p. xx.
165. Ephesians 5:11, *MSG*.

To divide life's activities into that which we perceive spiritual and secular not only disrespects the Creator, but devalues the one thing none of us seem to have enough of – time. All life is spiritual and time is the framework in which we get the opportunity to demonstrate God's kingdom through all of life's activities.

Just as a jeweller perceives the hidden beauty within an uncut diamond and cuts the gem accordingly, by perceiving the hidden value in every moment we handle time in a way that creates the minimum amount of wastage, carefully and constructively shaping our days to become a reflection of God's multifaceted grace, when recognising those moments of mismanaged time and calling on the author and finisher of time to help us retrieve what has been lost. For we are urged to be 'making the very most of your time [on earth, recognizing and taking advantage of each opportunity and using it with wisdom and diligence], because the days are [filled with] evil'. [166]

The word 'redeem' literally means to pay the price in order to 'buy back' something or someone that has been taken from us. In this way the Holy Spirit is calling us to become more intuitive, inventive, imaginative, industrious and entrepreneurial regarding our use of time; to stop wasting this most precious of commodities on trivial pursuits. For as third agers, we know all too well that time is running out.

Reflecting on an environment that daily bombards us with information, neuroscientist Susan Greenfield argues that the majority of which 'is the emotional equivalent to empty

---

166. Ephesians 5:16, AMP.

calories in junk food. In the name of staying connected we allow email, Twitter, Facebook and Instagram to capture our attention, but at what cost? Those empty calories gobble up our precious time'.[167] Maybe by altering our daily consumption of informational junk food, by parenting our phone usage and growing less dependent on social media, we will begin to maximise every passing moment.

Although in God's economy there is sufficient time to complete those works 'which [he] prepared beforehand',[168] it is our responsibility to manage the time we have. As Jesus said, 'I only do what I see the Father doing.'[169] To follow his lead requires us to become efficient operatives of the 'necessary no' and the 'essential yes'. By acting prematurely, refusing to move on, overstaying our welcome, going beyond the barbed-wire of those God-ordained boundaries, we rob ourselves of God's allotted timeframe. Saying 'yes!' to things, we have neither the time, energy, gifting or resources to do, has the potential to take us to breaking point. By refusing to be pressured by people, objects and events is to live in time and in tune with God's 'unforced rhythms of grace'.[170]

Time famine

Western society has every conceivable time-saving device at its disposal. Fast food, convenience stores, microwave meals, mobile phones, online shopping and drive-through

167. Samantha Boardman, MD, *11 Ways to Make the Most of the Time You Have*, www. happify.com (accessed 15.7.25).
168. Ephesians 2:10, ESV.
169. John 5:19, paraphrased.
170. Matthew 11:28-30, *MSG*.

outlets, to name a few. Yet instead of making us *time rich* we are increasingly becoming *time poor*. Twenty-first century living is suffering from an epidemic of what American psychologist Kathleen Vohs calls 'time famine'.[171] The more time we have, the more we want. Even with a plethora of time-saving devices, we seem to be starved of time.

Over and over again we hear people complaining that they have too much to do and too little time to do it in. Time famine has become a social disease of epidemic proportions. Affecting our physical, spiritual and emotional well-being, this perceived lack of time carries with it a number of undesirable side-effects. Physical tiredness, emotional fatigue and broken relationships can all be symptomatic of time famine. Even with endless gadgets and gizmos that are supposedly there to give us time to spare, we continue to suffer from time poverty.

Not that third agers are immune from this social virus. Often credited with having time to spare, many struggle to keep their heads above water. Feeling swamped by those endless demands on their time, seniors are constantly looking for ways in which to feed life's insatiable appetite for more time.

There is no panacea for the problem of time famine. The answer, however, is not more time, but to appropriate the wisdom and grace of God in a way that helps us manage time. As the biblical Solomon reminds us, 'For everything there is a season, and a time for every matter under heaven'.[172] As the author and finisher of time, God exists

---

171. Boardman, *11 Ways to Make the Most of the Time You Have*.
172. Ecclesiastes 3:1, ESV.

outside this time/space continuum. It is he alone who will ultimately help us to value, manage and redeem time. Our responsibility is to make the necessary adjustments that will enable us to complete our assignment within His timeframe.

When travelling between Chicago, USA to London, England, I would need to accept a different time zone and forward my wristwatch to reflect the six-hour time difference. Although my physical body clock might need a few days to adjust, my mind has to accept the time difference and act accordingly. By refusing to do so and trying to live the whole duration of the trip on American time would have created numerous problems. Missing pre-arranged appointments and the opportunities they present would potentially ruin the whole purpose of the visit. All because I failed to live in the reality of a time difference.

The New Testament uses two different words to describe *time*. The Greek word *Chronos* is the word from which we get the English term *chronometer* and *chronology*. The word talks of measured time, clock or calendar time. The other word for time is *Kairos*. This speaks of a special moment that may or may not have anything to do with either clock or calendar time. *Kairos* time is often referred to as God's time. The best way to illustrate their differences is to think in terms of the following scenario. 'About nine months or so into a pregnancy . . . many soon-to-be-mothers shake their husbands by the shoulder and say, "It's time!" He opens a bleary eye, looks at the clock, and says, 'It's 3:17 in the morning; go back to sleep!" She's on Kairos time, but he's talking Chronos. So, he gets shaken again: "It's time! And this time he gets it! IT'S TIME!!!"'[173]

Adam's rebellion in the Garden of Eden reversed the divine order, stamping humanity with a departure date. To counteract this catastrophic failure, God took on human form. In Christ, 'Time, which was created infinite, became finite.'[174] As the architect of time, Jesus showed us the necessity of living *in time* while helping us understand the need to live *through time*.

- **In Time** – Too live *in time* is to be fully engaged in the moment; to be physically, emotionally and mentally present. To be absent is to potentially miss out on those never to be repeated moments. A vacant look, filtered hearing, absent-mindedness or being distracted by 1,001 non-essentials could cause us to lose something or someone who will never pass our way again. A saying attributed to the ancient Greek philosopher Heraclitus is: 'Time is like a river. You cannot touch the same water twice, because the flow that has passed will never pass again. Enjoy every moment.' Time and timing are everything. To be out of time musically is to spoil the melody, whereas to be out of time mechanically is to lose the efficiency.

  To live *in time* is to be lost in the wonderment of the person, object or event. It's to enjoy the journey more than the destination. To appreciate a setting sun, a cascading waterfall, the vista of a magical

173. Guy Chevreau, *Catch the Fire: The Toronto Blessing* (London: HarperCollins, 1995).
174. Raynor, *Redeeming Your Time*, p. 6.

mountain range. To listen to symphonic birdsong. To give our full attention to a child who excitedly wants to tell us about their school day, when we have just experienced an eight-hour nightmare.

To live in *Kairos* rather than just *Chronos* time is to be in tune with the ongoing purpose of God. To be a living representation of the sons of Issachar, those described as 'men who understood the times, with knowledge of what Israel should do'.[175] Marching to a different drumbeat, these individuals lived in time, in tune and in touch with the affairs of heaven on earth. By knowing the inner prompting of the Holy Spirit, we can live 'in time' and 'through time'.

- **Through Time** – To live *through time* is to fundamentally realise that this life is but a minuscule micro-second in the light of a timeless eternity. To live *through time* is to live with an eternal destiny consciousness.

   Because '[God] has set eternity in the human heart',[176] there resides deep in the human subconscious a sense that we are created for more than this short, transient life. In his classic book entitled, *Eternity in their Hearts*,[177] author Don Richardson speaks of how God has prepared humankind to receive the gospel. From the jungles of Burma to the fortresses of Peru, through a variety of compelling stories, Richardson tells how even the most spiritually ignorant cultures

---

175. 1 Chronicles 12:32, NASB.
176. Ecclesiastes 3:11, NIV.
177. Don Richardson, *Eternity in Their Hearts* (Ventura, CA: Regal Books, 1984).

have an inherent concept of a Supreme Being. By awakening this inner consciousness of the eternal, the Holy Spirit enables a person to receive the good news of God's redeeming grace. For in all of us, there is a longing for immortality!

Although the futurist might fix their eyes solely on the far ground, we need to become spiritual landscape artists; those who observe the immediacy of the foreground, the lesser-defined middle ground, so as to see beyond the here and now towards God's prophetic horizon. For yesterday, today and tomorrow are all part of God's beautiful landscape called life. Living with *eternity in our hearts* enables us to focus on the future, while holding today and tomorrow in tension.

Living *through time* is to live prophetically, to be on the leading rather than the trailing edge of the affairs of heaven on earth, knowing that the enemy of living *in time* and *through time* is procrastination – to put off till tomorrow what should be done today. To become engaged in activities for which we were never intended is to fall prey of the diverting tactics of the enemy. Distractions are the enemy of time. To live in the moment is to appreciate that our time is limited.

Although the mastery of time is daunting, the best way to handle any gargantuan task is to break it down into bite-size moments. In this way time management becomes more manageable.

John Naber was the US high school backstroke swimming champion. Having watched Mark Spitz achieve seven gold medals in the 1972 Olympic Games, he immediately set himself a goal to win the gold medal for 100-metre backstroke in the 1976 Games in Montreal. The difference between his time and the world record was five seconds, which in terms of his perceived goal was gargantuan. Breaking down his target into what was nothing more than a bat-of-an-eyelid goal, he covered each of the four walls of his study with a twelve-month training regime. In 1976 Naber won the 100-metre backstroke, with a new world record of 55.49 seconds – 3.21 seconds faster than the previous record.

By caring for the hours, the days will take care of themselves. To become custodians of time we need to value, manage and redeem it. In so doing, with God's help, we make ourselves *time rich*, instead of *time poor*.

How time flies

'My eldest granddaughter has just graduated from University' – 'How time flies!'

'We've just celebrated our Golden Wedding Anniversary' – 'How time flies!'

'It must be fifteen years since I last saw you!' – 'How time flies!'

'Wow, is that the time, how time flies!' is a well-used closing statement on numerous conversations. While this idiom might be a valid excuse to exit an awkward situation, it has become something of a mantra for third agers.

Most seniors feel that time accelerates with age and the reality is they're not alone. As scientists delve into this strange phenomenon, their theories are varied. But all agree that as we age the difference between 'mind time' as measurable time and 'clock time' as perceived time becomes more evident. With the passage of time our memories increase and our perception of time changes. Whereas the young have few deposits in their memory bank, third agers have a plethora of memories on which they can draw.

In answer to the question: 'Why time speeds up as you age', Dr David R Hamilton writes:

> as we age, a year becomes a smaller fraction of entire lives up to that point. A year for a 5-year-old is one fifth (or 20%) of their life so far, but a year to a 50-year-old is one fiftieth of their life (or 20%) so it seems to pass ten times faster ... Time for an 80-year-old passes almost in the blink of an eye, sixteen times faster than it does for a 5-year-old.[178]

For each day of our lives, we are given 86,400 seconds. Our choice is how we value, manage and redeem those minute-measurements of time. Think of God in terms of a divine investor who each day deposits £86,400 or $86,400 into our bank account – an investment that needs to be used within a time period of twenty-four hours; anything left cannot be carried over to the next day or saved for a rainy day. What is not used is lost, wasted and gone forever. If this simple

178.   Dr David R. Hamilton, 'Why time speeds up as you age', March 17 2022, https://drdavidhamilton.com/why-time-speeds-up-as-you-age (accessed 24.7.25).

scenario occupied our thought process, would we behave differently regarding our daily allotment of time?

It is our responsibility to make the most of our allotted time, to live each day with an eternal destiny consciousness. To value this present moment as a pivotal point between our past and our future. For although time flies, we are the pilot.

Question marks!

- In what way do those Capuchin monks challenge our concept of time?

- Even retirees suffer from *time famine*, so how can we *make*, *share* and *give* time?

- If a diet of snacking on social media is the emotional equivalent to *empty calories* in junk food, how can we adjust our daily intake?

- How do you feel about every day being a divine investment of 86,400 seconds, for which God is looking for a return on his investment?

9

Missing Notes

When Mozart was a young man living at home with his father, Leopold, he enjoyed playing a little trick on his old man. After a night out in Vienna with his friends, Mozart would return home to find his father fast asleep. Mozart would then sit down at the family's piano and loudly play a rising scale of notes, only to stop one note short of completing the scale. Satisfied with the knowledge of what would inevitably come next, Mozart would go to bed.

As Mozart was falling asleep, Leopold would invariably begin to wake with the unfinished scale tossing and turning in his head. He couldn't bear the lack of resolution. Eventually, Leopold would drag himself out of bed, make his way to the piano, and play the last note. Only then could he go back to sleep.[179]

Whether we find Mozart's antics irritating or inspiring, the story is something of an allegory for living life in the last lane. Yet, to draw on its full potential, we need to relate to

---

179. Raynor, *Redeeming Your Time*, p. 24.

both the positive and negative aspects of this story. Just as the electronics of a traditional motor vehicle needs to connect with both the plus and minus terminals of a lead-acid battery, so it is with the motivational power found within the Leopold Mozart dynamic.

Negative niggle

With a sense of incompleteness tossing and turning in his mind and a single missing musical note messing with his brain, Leopold was awakened from his sleep. Only when he had completed the ascending musical scale could he find the peace of mind he so longed for.

Retirement is not always the respite people dream of. When an ageing mind begins to rehearse the ascending scale of life, retirees are awakened to the reality of life's missing notes. Unfinished tasks, failed aspirations, missed opportunities and mistakes made along the way arising from a chorus of 'should've', 'could've' and 'would've'. Negative thoughts that make third agers think of 'who they could have been but never became, and what they could have done, but never did'.[180]

In these critical moments, retirees run the risk of becoming victims of a 'Cinderella Syndrome'. With an overwhelming sense of mental servitude to past misdemeanours, we take on a scullery mentality, basement thinking that is inappropriate for the sons and daughters of a loving heavenly Father. Becoming inmates of a prison of our own making, the ugly

180. Erwin Raphael McManus, *The Last Arrow: Save Nothing for the Next Life* (Colorado Springs, CO: WaterBrook Press, 2017).

sisters of regret and remorse will undoubtedly come calling on a regular basis.

With the sound of life's unresolved issues resonating in our minds, the truth of Christ's redemptive work is all too easily silenced. To forensically acknowledge that we are destined to 'reign in life through one man Jesus Christ'[181] is not enough. Head knowledge is easily mugged by a gang of past misfits robbing us of the 'peace and joy in the Holy Spirit'.[182] Such comfort and celebration comes from heart knowledge. When failed hope and aspirations seek to mug us, only a radical rethink can silence the voices of intimidation and condemnation. We reject the lies of the enemy by 'reckoning'[183] or acting on God's eternal truth – to draw from our one-time spiritually bankrupt account and appropriate the truth that in and through a faith relationship with Jesus Christ we have ended our affiliation with failure. Rather than majoring on our insufficiency, we focus on Christ's all-sufficiency, remembering that we are 'complete in [him].'[184] For only by a renewed mind[185] are we able to renovate what the enemy's wrecking ball is constantly seeking to destroy – our state and standing in Christ. Satan is constantly seeking to bombard our minds with thoughts of personal failure. Yet to focus on our personal *performance* rather than our eternal *position* as sons and daughters of a loving heavenly Father is a negative niggle we can ill afford to play host to.

---

181. Romans 5:17, ESV.
182. Romans 14:17, ESV.
183. See Romans 6:11, KJV; 'reckon' – an accountancy term that means to take stock of what is financially available and to live within that reality.
184. Colossians 2:10, KJV.
185. Romans 12:2, NASB.

If music is the language of heaven, then our minds need to resonate with that glorious symphony of who we are in Christ. Eternity will host a celebratory ball to which Christ followers are cordially invited. A celestial event at which all things will find their ultimate consummation in Christ, an eternal moment when our heavenly Leopold will bring a full and final closure to all of life's missing notes.

While humbly acknowledging those mishaps, mistakes and missed opportunities made along the way, we need to take hold of our concerns and run headlong into the outstretched arms of a loving heavenly Father. Secure in the knowledge that 'There has never been the slightest doubt in [our] mind that the God who started this great work in [us] would keep at it and bring it to a flourishing finish on the very day Christ Jesus appears.'[186] For our eternal *position* should never be overshadowed by our earthly *performance*.

John Ronald Reuel Tolkien, author of *The Hobbit* and *The Lord of the Rings*, was one of the greatest novelists of the twentieth century. During the turbulent times of the Second World War, Tolkien's thoughts turned to the lack of time and whether or not he would have the wherewithal to complete his great work, *The Lord of the Rings*. These considerations culminated in him writing a short story entitled, *Leaf by Niggle*.[187]

Niggle was a painter who was constantly getting distracted by people, objects and events. Knowing that he would soon have to undertake a long journey (a metaphor for death), Niggle became obsessed with one particular painting. The canvas in question consisted of a vast

186. Philippians 1:3-6, *MSG.*
187. J.R.R. Tolkien, *Leaf by Niggle* (London: HarperCollins, 2016).

landscape with a large tree filling the foreground. Although the painting seemed over time to increase in size, the artist had a journey to make and time to complete his work was running out. Constantly fearing the work would never be finished, the time of his departure came and the canvas only consisted of a small leaf and a few surrounding details. Tolkien's story concludes with Niggle completing his long journey by entering what many believe was a metaphor of the afterlife. Here he sees his painting not only completed, but in some mystical way it had become the very landscape in which he was living.

That nagging niggle in all of us is best silenced by the understand that as Christ followers we are 'God's Masterpiece' a work of art which he has promised to complete.[188]

We all have a propensity to toss and turn with those missed opportunities, failed aspirations and unfinished tasks ringing in our ears. Having done what we can to play life's missing note, we need to place our trust in the founder and finisher of our faith[189] who will one day bring all things to completion.

Life in the last lane is all too often a reflective experience. When busy minds begin to rest, life's ascending scale begins to play. Each musical note becomes a memory. Some melodic, others discordant, each conspiring to create a mixture of thoughts and emotions. When these wild horses run roughshod through our minds, we need to corral 'every loose thought and emotion and impulse into

---

188. See Ephesians 2:10, Philippians 1:6.
189. See Hebrews 12:2.

the structure of a life shaped by Christ'.[190] When a sense of incompleteness disturbs our ability to rest in the finished work of Christ, we need to see our earthly *performance* through the lenses of our eternal *position*.

Paradigm shift

When it comes to the so-called 'sacred-secular divide', some would argue that this seemingly innocuous ideology that subdivides the Christian life into two halves of sacred and secular has subtilty infected people's view of age and the ageing process.

This belief system subdivides people, places and professions into two categories, each with different levels of importance and influence. Such ideology will ultimately minimise the affairs of heaven on earth. Those living with this distorted worldview might see their homes and local hostelry as *secular*, while church buildings are perceived as *sacred*. While pastors are placed on a *sacred* pinnacle, plumbers occupy a lesser *secular* role. All this, when in God's economy all life is sacred. All work, whether paid or voluntary, is worship. Ultimately, our calling, in whatever 'sphere of influence'[191] God places us, is a given opportunity to demonstrate the vision and values of God's kingdom in all we say and do.

Rather than advocating retirement, the New Testament focuses on lifelong service. When we secularise Christian ministry, our *calling* can be viewed as a *career* with a start-

---

190. 2 Corinthians 10:5, *MSG*.
191. See 2 Corinthians 10:13-14.

up and finishing time. In this way the human concept of retirement comes into play. All this when the 'calling[s] of God are irrevocable'.[192] God's call and commission is a lifelong commitment.

In whatever season or situation of life we find ourselves, whether the springtime of adolescence, the summer of adulthood or the autumn of elderhood, 'we are [God's] workmanship, created in Christ Jesus for good works, which God prepared beforehand so that we would walk in them'.[193] Following the example Jesus set, 'We need to be energetically at work for the One who sent me here, working while the sun shines. When night falls, the workday is over.'[194] Although we do not work for our salvation, we work from it. Our God-given assignment is a lifelong commitment. And whereas over time the vehicle may change, the vision remains.

On the road to Damascus, Saul experienced a dynamic conversion to Christianity; this resulted in him asking two fundamental questions, an enquiry that became a mantra for life:

Who art thou, Lord? ... what wilt thou have me to do?[195]

Resonating throughout his life, that yearning for spiritual intimacy was still evident in Paul's final years. In his sixties the apostle stated, 'I count all things to be loss in view of the surpassing value of knowing Christ' and 'that I may

---

192. Romans 11:29, NASB.
193. Ephesians 2:10, NASB.
194. John 9:4, *MSG*.
195. Acts 9:5-6, KJV; Acts 22:8-10.

know him and the power of His resurrection'.[196] Running in parallel with his cry for spiritual intimacy was his passion to fulfil his lifelong ministry. He said, 'I do not consider my life of any account as dear to myself, so that I may finish my course and the ministry which I received from the Lord Jesus'.[197]

In his book *The Last Arrow*, subtitled, *Save Nothing for the Next Life,* Erwin Raphael McManus writes:

> When you come to the end of your days, you will not measure your life based on successes and failures. All of those will eventually blur together into a single memory called 'life.' What will give you solace is a life with nothing left undone. One that's been lived with relentless ambition, a heart on fire, and with no regrets. On the other hand, what will haunt you until your final breath is who you could have been but never became and what you could have done but never did.[198]

There is a negative niggle in all of us and if a re-run were possible, we would possibly say and do some things differently. But living life in the last lane requires a daily resolve to leave nothing undone; in the spirit of our heavenly Leopold, to rise up and play those missing notes of which we are conscious, to pursue in life's 'little time' the purpose of God for which we were born. Turning the negative into a positive we become determined to complete

---

196. Philippians 3:8-11, NASB.
197. Acts 20:24, NASB.
198. McManus, *The Last Arrow.*

the call and commission received during our own Damascus Road experience.

Mirroring the will of heaven on earth, Jesus kept the main thing 'the main thing'. Without distraction or deviation from his prescribed pathway, he could whisper with his final breath, 'It is finished.'[199]

There is no more profound example of a man who left nothing undone, who held nothing back, who gave everything of himself and gave himself completely ... one word that let the world know you did exactly what you were born to do.[200]

Whether our lives be long or short, we need to live our time intentionally rather than casually, to complete the purpose for which we were born.

Leaving the best till last

In the opening verses of Joshua 13, God states the obvious. Speaking to the leader, Joshua, he says, 'You are old and advanced in years'.[201] Although *true*, the *truth* was that there was still much for Joshua to do. Probably in his late nineties his, like our, divine assignment was not age sensitive. Described as someone who 'left nothing undone of all that the LORD commanded Moses'.[202] Joshua never stepped away from his call or commission. When reaching

---

199. John 19:30.
200. McManus, *The Last Arrow*, p. 200.
201. Joshua 13:1, ESV.
202. Joshua 11:15, KJV.

what Western society perceive as 'retirement age' he is never heard saying things like, 'I've done my bit, let someone else take my place.' He refused to be sidelined from a divine commission which for him was a lifetime commitment.

Without sermonising the text, there are four character traits in the life of Joshua which all seniors should endeavour to subscribe to. Here is *fortitude*, someone whose courage and conviction would over time show him to be a man of *faith*. A leader, who for forty years humbly 'played second fiddle' to Moses. Just as the disciples of Jesus walked in the 'dust of their Rabbi' Joshua was a true servant-leader who showed himself to be someone who 'followed . . . fully'.[203] Add to this catalogue of character traits the fact that Joshua became a celebrated *finisher.* With dogged determination, he was someone who 'left nothing undone'.[204]

Among those biblical characters who in a spiritual sense aged well, we have people like Adam. Without concentrating on his catastrophic failings, living to age of 930, perhaps Adam's greatest achievement was a lifetime of caring for his wife and loving his God – never walking away from either. Enoch, in his 365 years on earth, was a man who 'walked with God'.[205] Abraham at the age of seventy-five took on a whole new commission, leaving a settled position to undertake the uncertainty of a nomadic lifestyle. As an elder statesman, at the age of 500, Noah took on an incredible building project. Isaiah and Daniel actively served God into their eighties and nineties proclaiming God's Word, no

---

203. Numbers 14:24, ESV.
204. Joshua 11:15, KJV.
205. Genesis 5:23,24; Hebrews 11:5, ESV.

matter what the cost. Simeon and Anna waited patiently for the fulfilment of God's promised Messiah. Anna, although in her late 90s, never felt more alive in the pursuit of God. Then we have the beloved disciple, John. Reckoned to be the youngest of the twelve, he outlived his companions. And over a lifetime that probably covered the whole of the first century AD, his passion for God's assignment never wavered. Although the secular world might perceive age to be a disqualifier, the divine composer sees the whole of life's symphony that builds towards a glorious crescendo.

Native to northern Mexico, the Agave Americana is known as a century plant. Typically blossoming at the end of its life cycle once every 100 years, only in the latter stages of life does it reach its full potential. Leaving this earth in a blaze of horticultural glory, the Agave Americana is truly a 'late bloomer'. It accomplishes its true reason for being in its final moments of life. What if for those experiencing their autumn years, our loving heavenly Father has kept the best wine till last?[206] That we are destined to be late bloomers? No matter how late the hour, with God's help we can reveal the beauty of Christ no matter our surroundings or circumstances.

Icolyn Smith, affectionately known as Ma Smith, was the founder of Oxford Community Soup Kitchen in the UK. In 1989 she saw a man eating from a rubbish bin and decided to do something about it. Using her retirement fund and her own pots and pans, she started up a soup kitchen. Up to the time of her death at the age of ninety-one, the kitchen had fed more than 45,000 people. Publicly confessing that she

---

206. John 2:10.

was driven by 'a love of God, a love of people and a love of helping',[207] Ma Smith was a classic later bloomer, someone who was fruitful in her 'old age'.[208] Sensing humanity's missing note, she blossomed in a way that revealed the love of God to those living within her community.

Ticking time bomb

In terms of human existence, the myths and mysteries of Eastern religions have created a different paradigm to Western thinking. With Hinduism, Jainism, Buddhism and Sikhism believing in reincarnation, those who follow these belief systems tend to be more relaxed about this life, believing they have many lives in which to get things done, whereas a Christian worldview believes we have but one life to live.[209] Each day is a priceless gift for which we are accountable. Living with an eternal destiny consciousness, the brevity of life causes Christ followers to march to a different drumbeat. Purpose-driven, they live each day so as to fulfil that reason for which God placed them on this planet.

The frailty of life tells us that human beings are by nature a ticking time bomb. The clock is ticking and the time of our ultimate departure has been set. Any one of us is only a phone call away from a doctor's diagnosis, a short sentence in which our hopes and aspirations come crashing down.

---

207. 'Ma Smith: Founder of Oxford Community Soup Kitchen dies aged 91', www.bbc. co.uk/news/uk-england-oxfordshire-63005821#:~:text=The%20founder%20of%20 an%20Oxford,man%20eating%20from%20a%20bin, 23 September 2022 (accessed 24.7.25).
208. Psalm 92:12-15, NIV.
209. Hebrews 9:27.

One hospital visit, and those beliefs we so boldly preached yesterday are unexpectedly mugged by a gang of thugs, whose only intent is to rob us of that peace that goes beyond all human understanding.[210] Overwhelmed by an unexpected set of circumstances, our thoughts are framed in the words of James: 'You don't know the first thing about tomorrow. You're nothing but a wisp of fog, catching a brief bit of sun before disappearing. Instead, make it a habit to say, "If the Master wills it and we're still alive, we'll do this or that."'[211] The fragility of life should cause us to build now, for the years we might not see!

The call no one wants

Hearing the nurse shout my name sent a chill down my spine. Whether a school classroom or a dentist's waiting room, I've always disliked hearing my full name being called out in a public, and none more so than this day. It was a Wednesday morning and along with my wife, we sat waiting to be ushered into the consultant's office. With a long list of patients, we had to wait beyond our appointed time. When the nurse eventually ushered us in, we could see the doctor was engrossed with his computer screen. He needed a few moments to update himself with the results from a variety of medical tests I had undertaken.

It was 10 June 2020 and we waited nervously to hear what the doctor had to say. Once the initial pleasantries had been concluded, the doctor turned away from his computer

---

210. See Philippians 4:7.
211. James 4:15, *MSG.*

screen and, looking me straight in the eye, said, 'I'm sorry, Mr Spicer, but you have cancer.'

As a child I well remember adults being so afraid to use the full word they preferred using the initial 'C'. Even today the so-called 'Big C' carries with it a severe health warning and a potential death warrant.

Twenty years earlier, my father had died from the same type of cancer. Then in 2018 my brother, seven years older than me, had passed away with the self-same diagnosis. In the years 2017-19 in the UK, 55,093 new cases and 12,039 deaths from prostate cancer were recorded.[212] Like it or not, I was now part of a national statistic, a hospital case number that would require further tests and possible surgery.

As the hospital consultant named the problem, along with assurances that the prognosis was good, the certainty that all human life is a ticking time bomb became a reality. An unwelcomed guest had come calling and much as I would want to ignore its advances, reality demanded that I acknowledged its presence. When death comes calling, the past becomes a treasure, the present a gift and the future an uncertainty.

As we near our final furlough, we're faced with the reality that even the most industrious person will one day take their final breath with unfinished tasks, failed aspirations, missed opportunities and mistakes made along the way, tossing and turning in their heads. However, we rest in the knowledge that all things will find their ultimate consummation in Christ. We therefore look to our heavenly

---

212. www.cancerresearchuk.org/health-professional/cancer-statistics/statistics-by-cancer-type/prostate-cancer (accessed 24.7.25).

Leopold to find a way to complete what we might believe is incomplete.

With amazing operas like *Madame Butterfly*, *La Boheme* and *Tosca* to his name, Giacomo Puccini is regarded as one of the greatest composers of his time. When in 1922 he was struck down with a terminal illness, he knew time was limited. His heartfelt passion was to compose one more opera; the opera in question was *Turandot*. When asked concerning the wisdom of commencing something he would in all probability never complete, he spoke of his conviction that what he had begun his disciples would finish. Following his death in 1924, his disciples did go on to complete the musical masterpiece. When premiered in Milan, Italy at Las Scala Opera House, under the skilful hands of Puccini's best student, the performance was stopped at the exact point Puccini had finished his work on the score. Turning to the audience, with tears streaming down his face, the student explained that this was where his master finished. Then with a beaming smile he picked up his batten and with singers and musicians alike completed what the master had originally conceived.

Mirroring the life of the biblical Joshua, third agers must maintain the same *fortitude, faith and followship*, in order to become a true *finisher*, knowing that if necessary, God will raise up others to complete our unfinished symphonies. But as long as we have breath to breathe, we will do whatever is necessary to leave nothing undone. With an attitude of fortitude, we endeavour to close out this life by:

- Leaving with zero offences;[213]
- Living intentionally not casually;
- Letting no person or events discourage or distract us;
- Finding and fulfilling our God-given assignments;
- Making God's call and commission a lifelong commitment;
- Leaving it all on the field of play.

---

213. Offences – caused by something said or not said, things done or not done.

Question marks!

- How should a Christ follower handle those negative niggles, those mishaps, mistakes and missed opportunities made along the way?

- Joshua was a man who 'left nothing undone'.[214] Is there anything you are putting off that you should be seeking to complete?

- Do you feel in tune and in time with the purposes of God for your life? If not, how do you intend to make adjustments?

- What are you building today for those tomorrows you may not see?

---

214. Joshua 11:15, ESV.

10

I've Started, So I'll Finish

Among the numerous framed mementoes hanging on my study wall, one in particular captures the essence of finishing well. The piece in question is an old, long-playing vinyl record along with its well-worn cardboard sleeve; it takes pride of place as a much-loved keepsake from the past. To the unobservant, it looks like something a record company might present to an artist to mark a particular sales milestone. But this piece of memorabilia has nothing to do with any commercial enterprise. The coloured photograph that forms the front cover of this particular record sleeve was taken more than half a century ago. Those involved in this photoshoot were either standing or seated around the steps of a large Edwardian country house in Surrey, England. Along with faculty and friends, the image incapsulates one undeniable truth that says: 'No matter how glorious our beginning, such splendour can easily fade in the light of how we finish'.

With its sea of smiling faces, the photograph is full of overwhelming optimism, capturing a moment in time when a group of passionate Bible college students looked longingly towards their future. Riding high on the adrenaline of dreams and aspirations, these twenty-somethings were poised for a life of possibility. Originating from various social, economic, ethnic and cultural backgrounds, the photographer had somehow managed to capture a body of starry-eyed, fiery zealots; people for whom the word 'impossible' had long been banished from their vocabulary. Here was a mosaic of abilities and personalities, young men and women, all naïve newbies to the world of Christian ministry. Having little idea as to what lay ahead, the world was their oyster, and with gritty determination, they were set on turning every obstacle into a pearl of wisdom.

Students and ships

Having been ushered through shipyard security into a highly sensitive military area, I stepped into a huge hangar on the edge of The Solent river in Southampton, England. Before me on the slipway was a gigantic, newly built Argentinian navy frigate. The atmosphere was electric. Passion and pride filled the air. As a military band played, high-ranking naval officers, politicians and shipyard managers mingled with the waiting crowd. Families, friends and invited guests stood looking up at this huge battleship-grey vessel towering over them. Everyone was eagerly awaiting the signal to launch. Long-standing dreams were about become a reality. No longer lines on a blueprint or sheets of steel on the shop floor, the visible evidence of years of planning and construction were about to be realised.

Following the customary bottle of champagne over her bow, the obligatory naming, along with a prayer of blessing, this ship was ceremonially commissioned. Slipping serenely into the water, this vessel was about to begin a lifetime in the service of the Argentine Navy.

The parallel between students and ships may not be immediately apparent, but both the Graduating Class of '69 and this naval frigate were about to begin a lifetime of active service. One for a heavenly government, the other for an earthly one. Both would undertake an ambassadorial role that could potentially take them anywhere in the world. While some might be called on to face conflict, others would spend a lifetime in a more serene setting.

Amidst all the celebratory hype surrounding each event, no one would have given a thought to the battles that lay ahead, the length of service each would offer and whether theirs would be a distinguished or disappointing career. Certainly, no consideration was given as to whether or not each would experience a glorious or ignominious ending to a lifetime of service. Wrapped up in the excitement of the moment, no thought was given to life's greatest challenge – Finishing Well.

Dr Robert Clinton, professor of leadership studies at Fuller Theological Seminary, some years back published an article entitled, 'Finishing Well: The Challenge of a Lifetime'. His research was based on 1,000 male biblical leaders. While some are only mentioned by their name and function, others had insufficient information to make a reasonable judgement as to how they had finished. But for leaders such as Moses, David, Paul and Jesus, there was much more data.

Of the 100 leaders Clinton found in-depth detail concerning their life, he could only come to a valid conclusion on half. While some died prematurely, others finished poorly and some had a mediocre finish. It was clear from his extensive investigations that few finished well.[215]

Looking back at that framed memento on my study wall, the majority of whom are now in their seventies and eighties, I would have to agree with Clinton's conclusions. The same pitfalls facing those Bible characters still lie in wait for today's unsuspecting leaders. The same challenges of financial irregularities, abuse of power, broken relationships, flawed character and spiritual plateauing are still relevant today. While some of my peers have passed away, others have either pulled up short or chosen to opt out of the race altogether. Yet, against all odds, a small minority of the Graduating Class of '69, most of whom the college principal categorised as 'those less likely to achieve' are still zealously pursuing their final furlong. All with a discipline and determination to *Finish Well*.

If it were possible to ask each of those graduating students about their passion to complete their race half a century on, I would suggest that everyone would echo the sentiments of Erwin McManus, when he writes: 'Imagine doing everything you were meant to do. Then, with a full heart, taking your final breath. That is a life fully lived . . . Never settle. It's all or nothing. Save nothing for the next life.'[216]

---

215. Dr J. Robert Clinton, 'Finishing Well: The Challenge of a Lifetime' (Altadena, CA: Barnabas Publishers Reprint, 1994).
216. McManus, *The Last Arrow*, Cover Flyleaf.

All's well that ends well

In Shakespearian speech, the phrase, 'All's well that ends well' is built around the concept of finishing well. However, while Shakespeare's play of the same name is seen as a comedy, for those Christ followers seeking to experience a glorious crescendo to life's third act, this is no laughing matter.

End-of-life-care has as much to do with our physical as it does with our spiritual and emotional well-being. To make that final push up the spiral staircase of life requires discipline and determination. When speaking of the end-game, the apostle Paul writes:

I'm not saying that I have this all together, that I have it made. But I am well on my way, reaching out for Christ, who has so wondrously reached out for me. Friends, don't get me wrong: By no means do I count myself an expert in all of this, but I've got my eye on the goal, where God is beckoning us onward – to Jesus. I'm off and running, and I'm not turning back.[217]

In terms of our earthly existence, the phrase 'Finishing Well' will mean different things to different people. For some it will mean relaxing at home, pursuing their hobbies, while others might visualise themselves sitting on some exotic beach enjoying a well-deserved rest. And for those fortunate enough to have a well-funded retirement plan, this is that moment in time in which they can complete their long-awaited bucket list. While for those caught up in

---

217. Philippians 3:12-14, *MSG*.

a consumerist mindset, *Finishing Well* is all about 'He who dies with the most toys, wins.'[218] Yet the more melancholy among us might bring everything down to a fundamental human desire for a swift and painless passing.

When those of a Christian faith consider their grand finale, their go-to text has to be Paul's words to his son in the faith, Timothy. Maybe hours away from martyrdom, the ageing apostle frames his final words as follows: 'The time of my departure has come. I have fought a good fight, I have finished the race, I have kept the faith. Henceforth there is laid up for me the crown of righteousness, which the Lord, the righteous judge, will award to me on that Day, and not only to me but also to all who have loved his appearing.'[219]

At a time when *'Holy Dissatisfaction'* is eroding and *'Holy Aggression'* is discouraged, Christianity risks becoming a melee of mediocrity. If such behaviour continues, the demise of a Christianity characterised by competitors running a race or combatant fighting a battle is imminent. When the apostle Paul used the word 'fought' he literally meant 'to engage in a conflict', either being used as a description of a *contestant* in a sporting event, or a *combatant* on the battlefield. In all probability being guarded by a Roman soldier on death row, Paul's words were more likely to refer to a combatant – elsewhere he likens our faith journey to an unnatural conflict, 'not ... against flesh and blood, but against principalities, against powers, against the rulers of the darkness of this age, against spiritual hosts of wickedness in the heavenly

---

218. Donald Sweeting, '*Finishing Well'*, www.nae.or/finishing-well (accessed 21.6.14).
219. 2 Timothy 4:7, *MSG*.

places.'[220] The Christian life is not a playground, it's a battleground.

Christians who want their final years to resonate with Paul's swansong will need to adopt a mantra that says: 'I'm a winner who sometimes loses, not a loser who sometimes wins.' For our end-game to be supernaturally successful, it will require adopting those two simple yet profound Pauline principles of Grace and Pace.

- **Grace**

   Of all the New Testament writers, the apostle Paul is for me the grace-man. From a dusty Damascus Road to the dank Roman prison cell, he became a living commendation of God's amazing grace. He more than most embraced this glorious gift, not merely in a cerebral way, but in a manner that was deeply spiritual and highly practical. As the 'Apostle of Grace', he lived his life under the umbrella of God's unmerited favour and heaven's supernatural ability.

   To finish our Christian journey in a blaze of heavenly glory will require us giving more than mere mental assent to God's grace. Head knowledge is not sufficient. Our identity, security, ministry, capacity and destiny are all wrapped up in our ability to embrace God's supernatural, all-sufficient grace. More than a one-time offer experienced at the point of conversion, God's grace is the undergirding foundation and the overarching focus of all we say and do. The apostle Paul makes this abundantly clear

---

220. Ephesians 6:12, NKJV.

when he categorically states, 'By the grace of God I am what I am',[221] for no matter my circumstances, '[His] grace is sufficient for [me].'[222]

That Christians *appreciate* God's grace as 'divine unmerited favour' that gives them undeserved access to God's redemptive plan, is wonderful.[223] Such could be seen as *transactional grace,* that has 'delivered us from the domain of darkness and transferred us to the kingdom of his beloved Son'.[224] But the grace narrative does not end there. Sadly, too many Christians fall short of appropriating the full revelation regarding God's grace. Grace is more than some spiritual nicety or a soft-centred delicacy in a box of ecclesiastical chocolates – a Christianised word verbalised in countless songs and endless religious conversations. Yes, God's grace should be *appreciated* as *divine favour,* but it also needs to be *appropriated* as *divine ability.* Something that could be understood as *transformational grace.* Heaven's supernatural ability that enables us to do what we cannot naturally do.

By taking hold of God's *saving* and *sustaining grace* in this way, our lives will reverberate with the lyrics of John Newton's well-known hymn.[225] Wordage that perfectly describes this Pauline principle:

221. 1 Corinthians 15:10, ESV.
222. 2 Corinthians 12:9, ESV
223. Ephesians 2:8.
224. Colossians 1:13, ESV
225. John Newton, 1725–1807, *Amazing Grace,* https://hymnary.org/text/amazing_grace_how_sweet_the_sound (accessed 16.7.25).

Through many dangers, toils, and snares
I have already come:
'tis grace has brought me safe thus far,
and grace will lead me home.

That is God's *transitional* and *transformational* grace in all its fulness. The wherewithal that enables every Christ follower to *Finish Well*.

- **Pace**

  The difference between finishers and non-finishers is based on two simple factors. The daily appropriation of God's amazing *grace* and the ability to maintain a sustainable *pace.*

  One of the best known of Aesop's Fables is the story of the Tortoise and the Hare, a tale about overconfidence verses consistency. While the Hare is a creature who is naturally fast and confident of winning every race it enters, the Tortoise is famously slow. Believing he was destined to win no matter what, the Hare stops running so as to take a rest and in so doing, falls asleep. The Tortoise, on the other hand, continues to move with a slow and steady pace towards the finishing line. It is the Tortoise that famously wins the race. The moral being: *The finishing line awaits those who consistently maintain a sustainable pace and do not become overly confident in their own ability.* For the Christian life is a marathon, not a sprint.

Most marathon runners who reach the finishing line will tell you that the hardest miles to run are usually eighteen through to twenty-three. While most competitors can run at a steady pace for the majority of the race, when overcome with physical fatigue and mental exhaustion, they hit an invisible wall. With their body and mind screaming to give up, it's at this critical moment that the divide between finishers and non-finishers is decided.

Like Paul, our confidence is not in our intellectual prowess, physical fitness, financial wherewithal or spiritual gifting, but in God's grace. Through his undeserved favour and supernatural ability, we are empowered to daily take incremental steps towards the finishing line. Only with heaven's help can we persistently push through those seemingly impenetrable obstacles that have the ability to discourage and ultimately disqualify us.

When the writer to the Hebrews picks up the analogy of the Christian race, he speaks of the need for 'endurance',[226] or what in modern terms might be called 'spiritual stickability'. Because without a sustainable pace, we run the risk of frying our emotions, abusing our spiritual gifts, damaging our physical bodies and neglecting those nearest and dearest to us. All this in that most honourable pursuits, 'the surpassing value of knowing Christ Jesus my Lord'.[227]

---

226. Hebrews 12:1, NASB.
227. Philippians 3:8, NASB.

Pacesetters and summiteers

Old age has the potential to become a lonely existence. For those determined to finish their race well, the need to engage the services of either a spiritual *pacesetter* or *summiteer* might seem obvious but not always possible. The individuals of which we talk are:

- Critical Friend;[228]
- People who value you and the goals you're aspiring to reach;
- Individuals sufficiently objective and provocative to be given permission to ask the difficult questions;
- More relational than task-orientated, they journey with you in a Christlike manner.

Those athletic runners who want to break the barriers set by previous generations will often engage the services of a *pacemaker*. Individuals with a proven track record willingly give their time and energy to help others achieve what they never will. By creating a winning pace for those coming after them, these pioneering individuals make a way in which someone else can follow. Gladly serving another person's dreams and aspirations, they inspire winners to become the best version of themselves they possibly can be. Theirs is a collaborative rather than competitive role,

228. *Critical Friend* – a supportive individual who believes in you and your goals enough to give much-needed constructive insight. Someone who has permission to disagree and give an alternative viewpoint.

sacrificing personal gain in order to celebrate in the success of others. Pacesetting has nothing to do with age, it's all about personal aspirations.

When thinking of famous pacesetters, the two names that spring to mind are Chris Chataway and Chris Brasher, two individuals known for their part in the epic race in which Roger Bannister achieved the first under-four-minute mile, a record-breaking run made possible by the efforts of his two faithful companions. Overshadowed by Bannister's record-breaking race, these often-forgotten runners helped what back in 1954 was seen as a superhuman athletic achievement.

Those observing this sporting spectacle speak of how with 275 metres to go, Banister kicked off from the pacesetter to manage the final 400 metre lap in fifty-nine seconds. There then followed a tantalising wait for the official time to be announced. Eventually Norris McWhirter, the stadium announcer, revealed that Bannister had crossed the finishing line in 'three minutes' – the cheering crowd of 3,000 spectators drowned out the 59.4 seconds. This sporting event goes down as one of athletics' great sporting achievements. All made possible by the inclusion of two pacesetters.

Twenty-first-century Christianity has a plethora of vacancies tailor-made for third agers; seniors willing to help the next generation to reach their potential; retirees willing to run their race with others in mind, fulfilling the role of a Critical Friend, these supportive, trustworthy, capable individuals are willing to sacrificially support the goals and aspirations of others.

Every climber attempting Mount Everest knows the importance of climbing with a recommended guide. As natives of the region, Himalayan Sherpas are known as 'Summiteers'. Being the most qualified, they have helped numerous individuals to reach the summit on multiple occasions. Some have died in the exercise of encouraging others to the zenith.

If .... summit, they themselves need to engage the services of a spiritual summiteer; critical friends who will journey with them through the challenges of life in the last lane. For the next generation to cross the finishing line, the reintroduction of godly pacesetters is a priority. With their experience, expertise, wisdom and know-how, third agers are well suited to pave the way for those coming after them. Herein lies the opportunity of a lifetime for those seniors willing to sacrifice their time and energy to enable others to run faster and reach higher than they ever thought possible.

I've started so I'll finish

The phrase 'It ain't over till it's over' is known as a 'Yogi-ism', taken from the life of the American baseball legend Yogi Berra; a British version would be translated as 'The Dunkirk Spirit'. It's an angle of approach to life someone adopts when the odds are against them; their backs are against the wall and the chips are down. It's a fighting spirit that pushes a person forward towards what potentially could be a glorious conclusion. In all its various forms, this phrase speaks of someone who refuses to give up on their dream and aspirations.

Writing about ninety-year-old Yogi Berra on the occasion of his death, journalist and author Gareth Rubin wrote:

There is something about the never-say-die, no-matter-the-odds-we-can-do-this spirit of 'It isn't over till it's over' that finds a place to inspire, time and time again.

It tells people to wait, don't make a judgement yet, because the struggle might be turned around ... What it does is remind you that there is still hope. That if you wipe the sweat from your brow, spit on the ground, and come out fighting, there is still a chance of triumph.[229]

---

229. Gareth Rubin, 'How people started saying "It ain't over till it's over"', 23 September 2015, www.bbc.co.uk/news/magazine-34324865 (access 16.7.25).

Rubin went on to Anglicise this Americanism by making the following humorous yet helpful quote: 'It ain't over until England get to the penalty shootout.'

For those struggling to scale those final steps on the spiral staircase of life, feeling as if the third act is too physically, mentally or socially demanding, the need to embrace such dogged determination is crucial. When faced with what Winston Churchill called 'This colossal military disaster' and the British nation being cornered with no apparent way out, Churchill raised an armada of small ships. With an attitude of 'It ain't over till it's over' he managed to evacuate nearly 400,000 troops from the beaches of Dunkirk.

By appropriating God's grace and maintaining a sustainable pace, those adopting this angle of approach to life refuse to be put off, put down or put out of the affairs of heaven on earth.

Gaining popularity from its frequent use by author, translator and journalist Magnus Magnusson, the phrase 'I've started so I'll finish' is self-explanatory. A catchphrase used during his twenty-five-year run as the television presenter of the British *Mastermind* quiz show, it was spoken whenever the time ran out while reading a question to the contestant. Almost autobiographical, 'I've started, so I'll finish' could so easily be a catchphrase for all our lives; a constant provocation to continue our journey of faith to its ultimate destination, no matter who or what tries to stop us. For as partakers of the divine nature, we are to mirror-image the Christlike character of 'he who began a good work in you will carry it on to completion'.[230] We

---

230. Philippians 1:6, NIV.

are not present in this moment to compete against others running the Christian race, our task is to complete our race no matter what happens along the way. One day we will all draw our final breath; the question is: 'Will we finish well?'

After the closing ceremony of the 1968 Mexico Olympic Games was over and all the awards had been given out, the spectators were asked to stay seated. Eighteen of the seventy-five marathon runners who began the race had already pulled out. The worthy winners, with their national anthems playing, had stood on the podium to received their gold, silver and bronze medals. Most thought the games were over. Everyone had finished except for the marathon runner from Tanzania, John Stephen Akhwari.

Halfway through this gruelling high-altitude race, Akhwari had fallen badly. Damaging his shoulder and dislocating his knee, he had every reason to pull up short. As night fell and the course was plunged into darkness, Akhwari pushed through the pain barrier. A little over an hour after the winners had finished, the Tanzania runner entered the Olympic stadium. Although the last man to cross the line, his prize was personal. Accompanied by police sirens and flashing lights, the runner from Tanzania hobbled into the stadium with his knee bandaged, to rapturous applause from the crowd.

Although he would not receive the prize for finishing first, to compete in and complete his race was reward enough. When asked why he didn't quit he simply said, 'My country did not send me 5,000 miles to start the race . . . They sent me 5,000 miles to finish the race.'[231]

---

231. www.olympics.com/en/news/marathon-man-akhwari-demonstrates-superhuman-spirit (accessed 24.7.25).

As ambassadors of heaven on earth, we push on to complete our God-given assignment, determined to cross life's finishing line with heavenly applause cheering us on and the accolade of a loving heavenly Father saying, 'Well done, good and faithful servant . . . Come and share your master's happiness!'[232]

232. Matthew 25:23, NIV.

Question marks!

- Is your present pace sustainable, or do you need to make some adjustments?

- Is your understanding of transactional and transformative grace in need of some recalibration?

- If 'Finishing Well' is the 'Challenge of a Lifetime', what safety nets are you putting in place to avoid becoming a non-finisher?

- Could you name someone who you see as a true 'Critical Friend'?

11

Sinking Bismarck

Although the steely-willed German chancellor Otto von Bismarck is known for his part in unifying Germany, his name is more often associated with a renowned Second World War battleship. Along with her sister ship, *Tirpitz*, these powerful war machines represented an evil Nazi ideology that pushed Britain to the brink of surrender.

However, before heading off down a rabbit trail thinking this chapter is some kind of verbal re-enactment of a Second World War naval battle, as fascinating as that might be, it's not. As important as the sinking of the battleship *Bismarck* was, we are simply using this historic event as a metaphor. A way in which to float a paradigm shift regarding a secular view of a season in life commonly referred to as 'retirement'.

More than 100 years before Bismarck was conceived, the 'Iron Willed Chancellor' launched a concept that would forever shape the course of Western social history. In the mid-nineteenth century, Otto von Bismack introduced a radical sociological idea. In an attempt to counteract high rates of youth unemployment, Bismarck proposed financial incentives for those seventy years of age and older to leave the workplace. Based on this initial idea, Western society has, over subsequent years, built a somewhat unilateral view of retirement. Whether it is the financial, sociological, physical or spiritual aspects of this departure from paid employment, this chapter proposes a very different vision for an age traditionally associated with withdrawal and even passivity.

On average, Baby Boomers are living three decades longer than their great-grandparents. While some over fifties are retiring from the workplace in what is being called 'The Great Resignation', others, because of financial reasons, are having to work into their late sixties and beyond. All of which is causing seniors to rethink how they will occupy the additional time and space life is giving them. Especially when Rick Warren, *The Purpose Driven Life* author, reminds us 'that the word "retirement" is not really a biblical concept . . . You may change jobs, you may change vocations and you may volunteer for free, but there is nothing that says you work most of your life and then get to be selfish for the next 20 years'.[233] With third agers now believing they have a key role in the affairs of heaven on earth, a secular ideology that dictates how people are expected to live out their final years no longer resonates with today's 'retirees'. All this when the Scriptures paints a very different picture. Addressing this apparent imbalance, Oz Guinness writes: 'We can retire from our jobs but we can never retire from our calling. Calling gives us our sense of task or responsibility right up to the last day we spend on

233. Stoyan Zaimov, 'Rick Warren Preparing for Humble "Retirement"', *Christian Post*, 22 March 2013, www.christianpost.com/news/rick-warren-preparing-for-humble-retirement.html (accessed 16.7.25).

earth, when we go to meet the Caller . . . We never retire from our calling . . . Our work may not last, but our calling never dies.'[234]

Believing that there is no biblical imperative for Bismarck's idea, this chapter unashamedly sets out to torpedo Western society's understanding of end-of-life activities. By attacking those social mindsets that sideline seniors solely on the basis of their age, we want to re-establish their rightful place in the ongoing purposes of heaven on earth. Returning to a biblical view of life in the last lane, this penultimate chapter seeks to restore the generational links that advocate a divine imperative for inter-generational communities.

Good idea or God's ideal

Google the word 'retirement' and your computer screen will soon be filled with images of silver-haired people gardening, playing golf, hugging their grandchildren or relaxing on some far-flung, exotic beach. All of which creates a somewhat idyllic view of how people hope to spend their final years. But this somewhat utopian view of retirement is something of a 'Never-never land' which seniors may or may not manage to enjoy.

The most dangerous year of our adult life is the year we retire. Whether it's the loss of purpose or becoming less physically and mentally active, we all need a purpose that reaches beyond our so-called retirement. The reality is that people of all ages are having to rethink how they will occupy the additional space being created by an increased

---

234. Bob Buford, *Finishing Well* (Nashville, TN: Integrity Publishers, 2004), pp. 247, 250.

life expectancy. Whether it's to supplement their income, regain the loss of workplace camaraderie or rediscover their reason for being, some retirees are choosing to either return to the workplace or give their time to volunteering.

While some are enjoying the whole retirement experience, others are finding the second half of life is not all it's cracked up to be. Or as Professor Teresa Amabile of Harvard Business School concluded, 'While retirement might start off in a blaze of well-deserved relaxation the novelty can soon wear off'. She goes on to challenge her retirees, 'to think about who [they] will be – who [they] want to be when [their] formal career ends.'[235]

Although what Otto von Bismarck conceived was initially seen as a good idea, J.I. Packer aggressively dismisses the whole retirement concept as being non-biblical:

> Retirees are admonished, both explicitly and implicitly, in terms that boil down to this: Relax. Slow down. Take it easy. Amuse yourself. Do only what you enjoy. You are not required to run things anymore, or to exercise any form of creativity, or to take responsibility for guiding and sustaining goal-oriented enterprises. You are off the treadmill and out of the rat race. Now, at last, you are your own man (or woman) and can concentrate on having fun . . . So now go ahead and practice self-indulgence up to the limit . . . As far as society is concerned, you are now on the shelf.[236]

235. Ian Rose, 'Why we lie about being retired', 20 August 2019, www.bbc.co.uk/news/business-48882195 (accessed 16.7.25).
236. J.I. Packer, *Finishing Our Course with Joy: Ageing with Hope* (Nottingham: IVP, 2014), p. 27.

If Christianity persists in advocating this secular philosophy, it could inadvertently set the scene for a 'silver riot'. A moment in time in which seniors will humbly voice their concerns regarding their unfulfilled hopes and aspirations. Unhappy with the present state of affairs, older people are now seeing that they have a key role in the purpose of heaven on earth. This cultural and attitudinal shift means that while some retirees may prefer to spend their time relaxing at home pursuing their hobbies, others are looking for a more adventurous way of life. For while our *career* may end, our *calling* never does.[237] Our career may evolve over time, but the one constant in an ever-changing world of work is the call and commissioning of God. That call will trump our career every time. No matter where our present sphere of influence might be, our assignment as ambassadors of heaven on earth has no best-before date attached. Retirement is a state of mind, not a state of play.

Rather than talking of retirement, the New Testament advocates lifelong service. Those seeking a biblical basis for Bismarck's ideology will undoubtedly point to one particular Old Testament reference. But rather than validating the classic view of *retiring*, this scripture advocates a *repositioning, repurposing* and *re-engaging* of third agers into kingdom activities.

- **Repositioning**

  Those looking for a foothold on which to establish their retirement philosophy only have Numbers 8:23-26 to cling to. Here we read of the Levitical

---

237. Matthew 28:19-20

priesthood entering the service of God as vibrant twenty-somethings: young men called to maintain and minister God's work within a place of worship, known as the tabernacle. To work within the confines of what was a glorified tent, they needed to be able to carry out work that was physically demanding. Having entered the priesthood at the age of twenty-five years old, priests were required to cease certain aspects of the work that required heavy lifting or close inspection.

Some historians *would* say that this upper age limit was put down to practical issues, such as physical strength and fading eyesight. Without the aid of optical lenses, elderly priests would struggle to inspect those with skin disease. 'Virtually no one over the age of fifty would be able to see anything at close range.'[238] In the apparent role reversal, older priests served their young counterparts; it was not a *removal* from but a *repositioning* to. Rather than redundancy, this was a God-ordained reassignment within the redeemed community.

No longer involved in the heavy lifting or the close inspection of diseased people, the over-fifties were transitioned to a place where they would '*assist* their brothers in performing their duties at the tent of meeting'.[239] This 'was not to *remove* productive workers from service, but to *redirect* their service in a more mature direction'.[240] Certain duties would

238. Numbers and Work, www.theologyofwork.org/old-testament/numbers-and-work/ (accessed 16.7.25).
239. Numbers 8:26, NIV, emphasis mine.
240. www.theologyofwork.org/old-testament/numbers-and-work/ (accessed 16.7.25), emphasis mine.

become the responsibility of younger priests, while the over-fifties transitioned to a different form of service. For the old to serve the young was never meant to be derogatory or demeaning!

The word 'assist' describes the function of the over-fifties who with a servant heart, *work with* and *wait upon* others. Rather than thinking in terms of 'lowly ranking', we should think of a 'loving relationship'. The same word is used for a young Samuel, '*ministering* to the LORD under Eli'.[241]

Just as a master craftsperson stands alongside their apprentice to *assist* them in learning a new skill, or a nurse *ministers* to those in need, a *waiter* serves tables, or an *attendant* makes themselves available to serve others, the older priests were repositioned to serve younger priests. They assisted in a way that would encourage, equip, empower and embolden their protégés to become all that God intended them to be. Herein is the true essence of servant leadership. Seniors coming alongside their younger counterparts to 'assist their brothers' in their recognised ministry in God's house.

Some would even suggest that it was these elderly Levities who sat at the city gates, taking up a position in which they would offer a listening ear, wise counsel, instruction and warnings to those living within the city walls. When the Levitical priest Eli was in his nineties, his former duties within God's house had long since ended, and he was found sat

---

241. 1 Samuel 3:1, ESV, emphasis mine.

on 'his seat by the side of the gate'.[242] As an older statesman Eli made himself available to dispense Godly wisdom to others. In an elderly Eli we see how twenty-first century senior saints should position themselves as 'elders at the gate'. Not retiring, but re-positioning themselves to give assistant to their younger counterparts along with a listening ear, wise counsel and instruction to those who requested it.

- **Repurposing**

Living in a throwaway society that has forgotten the environmental covenant God established with Adam, Christianity should be taking the lead in stewarding creation. Hard to believe but maybe the Greta Thunburgs of this world are a prophetic wake-up call to a generation guilty of crimes against the environment. The amount of waste the average Westerner creates is staggering. But sadly, there is another kind of wastage taking place within the realms of Christendom that is equally disturbing. To observe the way in which seniors are discarded and thrown away as no longer needed is a tragedy of gargantuan proportions. The expertise, experience, wisdom and knowledge that elderly Christians carry is immense. Yet somehow one-dimensional leaders are failing to see those hidden assets that sit in front of them on a weekly basis. For those who dismiss this as nonsensical, they should consider this: When

---

242. 1 Samuel 4:18, see also verse 13.

the elderly die, a library is lost and those volumes of wisdom and knowledge are gone forever!

No wise investor would ever think of entrusting wealth in something or someone that would then be wasted. A return on kingdom investments is part of the divine DNA. If proof were needed, we should perhaps re-read the New Testament parable of the talents.[243]

However, the other side of the coin is that third agers could be guilty of behaving in a way that is tantamount to burying the light of their experience, expertise and wisdom under the retirement bushel. To take ourselves out of the game is a failure of understanding the divine intent of reflecting God's glory through the prism of an inter-generational Church.

The art of repurposing seniors is perhaps best seen in the ancient custom of rejuvenating 'old wineskins'. Used to store water and wine, these containers, being made of animal skins, were liable to harden, crack and leak with age. Although some might discard them as being past their best-by-date, the savvy individual would see treasure in what others perceive as trash. With longevity in mind, they would soak the hardened wineskin in oil so as to remove its rigidity and restore its flexibility. Revitalising the old with fresh oil, these items were repurposed so as to carry refreshing water to the thirsty, or revitalising wine to the weary. The spiritual parallels of this

243. Matthew 25:14-30.

prophetic act are self-explanatory and call on us to pray for the restorative nature of a loving heavenly Father to return to twenty-first-century Christianity.

To become fixated on human traditions and old paradigms, the elderly run the risk of losing their spiritual usefulness. To allow the person of the Holy Spirit to daily overtake our inability with his ability is the only way third agers can be repurposed so as to carry the refreshing Word of God to a thirsty world.

- **Re-engaging**

Speaking of the need for seniors to re-engage into today's society, Henry George asks a pertinent question:

> Where did all the adults go? Why, when the chips are down and some new cooked-up controversy over our culture, society and our very identity arises, do those in positions of power and authority, the grown-ups, leave the field? . . . The lack of an adult perspective means that our leadership class is rudderless, our intellectual class is visionless, our cultural elites are valueless, and our financial elites are shameless. Today's young are existential orphans, looking around for guidance and boundaries within which they can orient themselves.[244]

---

244. https://mallarduk.com/generation-orphan-how-our-society-lost-adulthood-and-its-future-henry-george/ (accessed 16.9.22).

When ageing voices are no longer heard, a generational crisis will begin to emerge. The absence of adult influence on any society will create a culture in which immaturity rules and ineffectiveness follows. Within this human environment common sense, common decency and common courtesy are no longer common. Hence the need for intergenerational communities,[245] an environment in which young and old engage with each other. Not some spiritual experiment in which, for one hour on Sunday morning, we play-act and pretend that we are doing life together. But a setting in which all ages truly relate to and value one another. A deeply spiritual and empathic environment in which the success of one is the success of the other.

Old people can often see young people making mistakes and stumbling through life ignorant of the consequences of their choices. As much as we may want to look away and leave them to their own devices, God repeatedly seeks to instil in those with wisdom and experience a sense of duty towards those without it.[246]

Sir Walter Raleigh became one of the most celebrated explorers of the first Elizabethan era. In Sir John Everett Millais famous painting entitled *The Boyhood of Raleigh*, Raleigh is shown as a young boy listening attentively to the wonderful stories being

---

245. Deuteronomy 6:5-9; Exodus 13:8-16; Joshua 4:4-9; Psalm 78.
246. www.thetrumpet.com/17290-young-and-old-together (accessed 16.7.25).

told by an older Genoese sailor. The artist placed a toy ship in the foreground, to seemingly speak of Raleigh's future adventures, prophetically pointing to a day when this English statesman would become an explorer extraordinaire. Highly favoured in the royal courts, he would discover yet unknown territories.

A life lived is a life shared. More than any other time in history, Christianity needs a spiritual version of 'Genoese sailors', seniors who will inspire the next generation, creating in them a sense of divine adventure. Knowing that they are highly favoured in the courts of heaven, they come to 'know their God and do exploits for the kingdom of heaven on earth'.[247] To launch out into the depths of godly revelation by refusing to paddle in the shallows of present-day Christianity, no longer fearfully hugging yesterday's shoreline, they dream of undiscovered territories awaiting those bold enough to set sail into God's supernatural sunset.

The young need to be understood, not condemned. They need pivotal people in their lives who will stand in the generational gap and encourage them to go further and faster than the old ever thought possible.

Inter-generation communities

We thankfully acknowledge those Christian communities who are seeking to move beyond the margins of being

---

247. Daniel 11:32, paraphrased.

monogenerational churches solely set on attracting a young clientele. However, before congratulating ourselves on achieving a *multigenerational* congregation in which a mixed age group gather, we need to delve a little deeper. When speaking of silo-mentality towards seniors, Jay Blunt writes, 'typically, the church caters to the elderly with small trips, social events, luncheons, camaraderie, and book discussions. Certainly these help alleviate the loneliness that older people often face.' [248] Then quoting J.I Packer he concludes that this is 'one of the huge follies of our time'.[249]

If church congregations become so youth-centric that other age groups are made to feel unwelcome or unwanted, the body of Christ can no longer be said to truly represent the heart of a loving heavenly Father. Just as racism is an afront to the gospel, so is ageism. When middle-aged worship leaders are 'encouraged' to step aside so as to be replaced by their younger counterparts for no other reason than to look 'relevant' and 'cool,' then the future is flawed. When being cool overtakes being Christlike, Christianity has stepped onto a downward spiral of no possibility.

New Testament communities were *inter-generational*, spiritual environments in which young and old listen and learn from each other. It was a culture in which the old and young had a mutual respect and enjoyed real spiritual relationships with each other.

To anaesthetise the Church to the key role third agers play is tantamount to creating a sleeping beauty that needs the divine kiss of life. In the same way, to restrain the young

248. Ray Blunt, *Elders at the Gate* (Leicester: WordCrafts Press, 2018), p. 22.
249. J.I. Packer, *Finishing Our Course with Joy*, p. 29.

from strategising the way ahead will hamstring the body of Christ. To create an environment in which young and old flow together is to build *inter-generationally.*

Using his maiden speech to introduce the Holy Spirit as the executor of God will on earth, Peter, on the day of Pentecost, spoke of the end-time Church in which 'your sons and your daughters shall prophesy, and your young men shall see visions, and your old men shall dream dreams'.[250] Here is an inter-generational environment in which young visionaries and elderly dreamers flow together and phenomenal growth is experienced.

Coffee gate

There has perhaps never been a more significant moment in Church history when the term 'elders at the gate'[251] is more relevant than now. The phrase speaks of a time when:

> the city gate was where people went for judicial decisions, for counsel, and to gather the latest news. Those who were no longer able to go off to the fields, to their shops, or to the market to work, spent much of their time sitting by the gates of the city. They assumed their places as other elders had before them, taking up their necessary roles reserved for them. This was a societal position, one expected of them as they became

250. Acts 2:17, ESV.
251. At the city gate Lot sat waiting for an angelic visitation – Genesis 19:1; Wisdom sits in the gate – Proverbs 1:21; Family issues are resolved – Deuteronomy 21:18-19; Important civil business conducted – Genesis 19:1; Marriage issues sorted – Ruth 4:1-13; Kings ruled and gave instructions to their troops – 2 Samuel 18:1-5 compare 19:1-8.

the next keepers and dispensers of judicious wisdom to the coming generations.[252]

The biblical term 'elder' can mean different things to different people. On the one hand it can simply be descriptive of those who live a long life and therefore speaks of *age*. With extended years comes accumulated experience, expertise, wisdom and know-how on which people can draw. The term can also speak of the inherent *ability* of those who have graduated from the university of life. But in New Testament terms, the word 'elder' not only speaks of *age* and *ability*, it speaks of Holy Spirit *anointing* and *authority* – the legal right to rule. Those called to church eldership are supernaturally set aside by the Holy Spirit to act as spiritual parents who exercise rule in God's house.

Twenty-first-century Christianity needs seniors to position themselves as elders at the gate! As a third ager, 'city gates' have for me transitioned into what could best be called 'Coffee gates'. History teaches us that coffee chats can change the course of social history. It was the coffee houses of Paris that sheltered revolutionaries plotting the storming of the Bastille whereas today they host would-be authors plotting their latest book. During the Age of Enlightenment, the coffee house fuelled the philosophy of people such as Voltaire, Rousseau and Isaac Newton. Coffee shops fired revolutionaries, fuelled the Enlightenment and furnished entrepreneurs with an environment to discuss their ideas; 'coffee gate' comes from a good pedigree. In the Ottoman Empire, coffee drinking became a capital offence for which

---

252. Blunt, *Elders at the Gate*, p. 2.

the death sentence was decreed. Yet coffee was such an integral part of social history that in Saudi Arabia the failure to supply your wife with coffee was 'grounds' for divorce.

Coffee shops are, for me, an environment where coffee is drunk and 'gate-worthy wisdom' is shared. Here older people listen and learn from their younger counterparts and vice versa. Here is a place where third agers can be *repositioned, repurposed* and *re-engaged* in the affairs of heaven on earth. Here is where I get the opportunity to enjoy a two-way conversation with young male spiritual revolutionaries. Never wanting to come across as an arrogant know-it-all who seeks to download information on some unsuspecting individual, it is here that two learners do life together. Time at the gate should of necessity involve a conversation that is priestly, pastoral and prophetic.

These are moments in time in which I get to ask God to give me the grace to inspire those young 'spiritual Raleighs' to embark on godly adventures. Coffee gate is where inter-generational conversations take place and spiritual transformation is experienced!

Steve Phifer puts it perfectly when he writes, 'We need the gates and the elders . . . not to criticize but to encourage the young ones – to fan the flames of their devotion to Christ and to speak eternal things into their lives. We must trust the Holy Spirit to lead them, as He did us, to apply the eternal things to their generation.'[253] Socially and spiritually humanity is in danger of losing its 'city gates'. 'The young need anchoring in deep, adult connections; their elders need to rediscover their established purpose in their last lap – together they can restore the broken links of the design for a full, meaningful life as intended by their creator.'[254] Sadly, the prophet Jeremiah's lament resonates with today's world when he says, 'The elders no longer sit in the city gates; the young men no longer dance and sing.'[255]

If there was ever a time in which the 'Nehemiah spirit' needs to re-emerge, it is now. The 'city gates' are in ruins and seniors need to mourn their loss, for:

without city gates, perhaps we have lost something we didn't even know we were missing; something essential to a good life even – a place to go for wisdom, a purpose to fulfil for those who are ageing, an accessible and established link to the generations that follow

---

253. 'Elder at the Gate', stevephifer.com/elder-at-the-gate/ (accessed 16.7.25).
254. Ibid.
255. Lamentations 5:14, NLT.

. . . Where do those younger generations go for wisdom today? Google; Wikipedia; YouTube for starters. That's about the size of it. What is the purpose for those who have years of life ahead? Retirement? Golf? Fifty-five and over are perpetual care communities?[256]

Rather than seeing an emerging generation as an obstacle, seniors need to see them as an opportunity. This is a prophetic moment when third agers need to stop sitting on the sidelines reminiscing about the 'good old days'. This is our time and our turn to find our own version of 'coffee gate', to engage with, encourage and empower the next generation to embark on a godly adventure.

---

256. Ray Blunt, *Elders at the Gate*.

Question marks!

- What are your thoughts on the statement: 'Retirement is a state of mind, not a state of play'?

- What would your version of 'coffee gate' be?

- How do seniors avoid becoming like 'old wineskins' – hard, inflexible and broken?

- Are inter-generational churches a pipedream or a necessary reality?

12

Never Let the Old Man In

Clint Eastwood is forever locked into my childhood memory as the character Rowdy Yates in the 1950's television Western Series *Rawhide*. Others will more readily associate his acting career with films like *A Fistful of Dollars* (1964), *Where Eagles Dare* (1968), *Dirty Harry* (1971), *In the Line of Fire* (1993) or *The Mule* (2018). With a long list of classic movies to his name, this multiple award-winning Hollywood superstar has for well over half a century entertained cinema-goers the world over. Love or loathe his movies, it's not so much his acting career that the elderly envy, but his ability to make the ageing process look so easy. Attempting to crack the 'Eastwood Code' for ageing well, journalist Lauren Russell writes

> The 91-year-old who has achieved endless success within Hollywood has also achieved remarkable success in fighting off the effects of ageing. What is the star's secret to living a long life? With four Oscar awards and four Golden Globe awards to his name, Eastwood has had a lifetime of achievements. But away from the screen, what many adoring fans wish to know

is how Eastwood handles life as an ageing citizen and what lifestyle habits he follows to have gotten him to his 90s.[257]

To delve deeper into Eastwood's philosophy of age and the ageing process is to hear him speak fondly of an old friend. Enquiring as to how this ninety-year-old colleague manages to look and act so good for his age, Eastwood says:

> 'I have a friend that is in his 90s, and I said to him, "You look really good – what's the deal?"' To which his friend responded with a one-liner so incredibly simple, yet so profoundly sublime. His answer was simply: 'Never let the old man in'. Six words which Eastwood concluded, 'And he never did.'[258]

Growing old outrageously

Over recent years I have begun to wonder whether growing old outrageously has gone out of fashion and if so, is it time for a revival. Having grown up within conservative Christian circles, breaking with convention does not come easily. But, here's the question – has Christianity created a stereotypical view of seniors? Does the Church have a cookie cutter approach to retirement? Is there a one-size-fits-all view of those living life in the last lane? If so, would embracing

---

257. Lauren Russell, 'Clint Eastwood health: Actor on 'Eastwood Code' that maintained his health for 91 years', www.express.co.uk/life-style/health/1535310/clint-eastwood-health-long-life-secret-healthy-eating-exercise (accessed 16.7.25).
258. Russell, 'Clint Eastwood health'.

a non-traditional or unconventional approach to age and the ageing process be wrong? Have we so standardised old age with an unspoken set of expectations that to look, act or live differently is viewed as shocking? If so, then count me in. For if living life to the full seems a little eccentric, continuing to pursue our passions a little extreme and trying new things somewhat outrageous – then growing old outrageously gets my vote.

What if God intended spiritual exploits to remain within our remit? To engage with the supernaturally unexpected and embrace God-inspired adventures by defying the stereotypical view of old age was all part of God's agenda? For when citizens of God's kingdom revert to type and become the classic male curmudgeon or cantankerous old lady, they fail to become the unique one-of-a-kind individual that God intended.

Old age is a generational tightrope walk to which the young rarely give any thought. A precarious high-wire act that involves discipline, resilience, focus and preparation, all while monitoring and maintaining our mental equilibrium. An art traditionally associated with the circus, tightrope walking like old age is an uncertain journey between two fixed points. A balancing act, which given the choice, few would engage in. Even though surrounded by family and friends cheering us on, this solitary high-wire act is a course of action for which there is no practise run. Trying to maintain our balance when physical, social, financial and spiritual pressures are trying to throw us off course is a challenge third agers face on a daily basis.

Whether we fantasise about finding the elixir of eternal youth or subconsciously harbour the Peter Pan Syndrome, last-lane living demands that we find the balance between acting as either antiquated antiques or recycled teenagers. The only way to traverse life's tightrope successfully is by maintaining a Christlike attitude; an angle of approach to life outlined in the ancient Christian text known as the Bible.

Age is an attitude

When involved in any conversation regarding age and the ageing process, some conversationalists will make a pre-emptive strike by stating that 'Age is just a number'. My immediate response would be that 'Age is an Attitude'. While age as an arbitrary number centres on the passage of time, age as an angle of approach to life speaks of a personal belief system with which we choose to monitor and maintain our rightful place in the affairs of heaven on earth.

No matter how we factor in life's third act, there is always an older version of us trying to gain access. We all know individuals who, despite their chronological age, refuse to let the passage of time define them. Then there are those who think, act, talk and dress older than they actually are. All because they have allowed an older version of themselves to gain access into their way of thinking. No matter what gene-pool our parents fished in, a youthful outlook on life has more to do with our attitude than it does with our DNA.

There is an old biblical Proverb that says, 'As [a person] thinks within [themselves], so [they are].'[259] Flying in the face of popular opinion, we are not what we *eat* or what we *wear*, we are the sum total of what we *think*. For, what we *believe* affects how we *behave* and ultimately what we *become.* Just as a pilot adjusts the angle of approach of an aircraft to create a successful take-off or landing, our mental attitude towards the ageing process will either cause us to soar and 'reign in life through the one man Jesus Christ'[260]

259. Proverbs 23:7, NASB.
260. Romans 5:17, ESV.

or create a scenario in which we physically, emotionally and spiritually crash and burn.

The America's Cup is to yachting what the Ashes are to cricket or the Super Bowl is to American football. So, imagine the dismay felt by the USA skipper Dennis Conner, when he lost 'their cup'. Having been granted the privilege of representing his country, Conner had committed the gravest possible offence, by losing the cup to the Australians for the first time in its 132-year history. Over the next four years, the defeated skipper set about restoring his country's pride and his own reputation. He searched for ten men, from the hundreds available to him, to create a winning team. He made it clear that 'no one would make the team unless he put winning the cup ahead of everything else in his life'. Seven days a week, up to eighteen hours a day, Conner prepared himself, his crew and his boat for the ultimate challenge. When asked about the three major factors that characterised a successful crewmember, he replied, *'Attitude, attitude, attitude.'*[261] As John Maxwell points out attitudes become, 'the librarians of our past, the speaker of our present (and) the prophet of our future.'[262]

The truth is that although we're born with zero mental attitudes, we all harbour a cluster. Built around our past education, experience and environment, over time these attitudes become:

- Silent jurors ready to bring a judgement on people, objects and events;

261. Dennis Conner, *Comeback: My Race for the America's Cup* (London: Bloomsbury Publishing, 1987), p. 65.
262. John Maxwell, *The Winning Attitude* (Nashville, TN: Thomas Nelson, 1993), p. 24

- Lenses through which we view life, creating our personal perspective;

- Learned responses;

- Frames of reference through which all incoming experiences are measured.

It's no accident that while some seniors seem to soar above the challenges of life, others seem to struggle under a cloud of circumstances. While some manage to maintain a winning edge despite the passing years, others resign themselves to life on a downward spiral of no possibility. All too often, a poorly adjusted mental attitude becomes the source of the problem.

When it comes to adjusting or altering our angle of approach to age-related issues, we need to understand the composite parts of those mental attitudes that affect our daily lives. Whether they are true or false, our *beliefs* form the basis of every mental attitude. Therefore, any noticeable change regarding our angle of approach to life will involve a change of thinking. For those internalised beliefs that consist of generalisations, stereotypes, imaginations, assumptions, fears and prejudices never lay dormant. Left to their own devices they will affect our *feelings*, which in turn will ignite either a negative or positive *reaction*. We can alter our lives by adjusting our attitude.

Old before our time

Before he died, a widower friend of mine unknowingly gave ample proof as to the power of the phrase, 'Never let the old man in.' In his sixties he fell in love and married a wonderful Christian lady, twenty-five years his junior. Besides the social challenges their marriage created, it was fascinating to observe the way in which their beliefs and behaviour developed over time. Wondering how the age difference would relate to their relationship, I fully expecting the young lady to keep the older gentleman youthful in his outlook on life. However, the reverse happened. Either to mask their age difference or seeking to make their relationship more socially acceptable, over time his younger partner began to think, talk, dress and behave as someone twice her age. Her language and lifestyle began to marry up with her older partner. She had unknowingly let an older version of herself gain access.

Not that anyone is advocating that seniors dress or act like recycled teenagers, attaching some kind of hip hop language to their vocabulary or styling their hair (if they still have any) in accordance to the latest fashion craze, because that would be just plain weird. Trying to cheat the biological ageing process says more about our attitude, than our appearance!

Those who change their belief system so as to maintain a progressive mindset towards the ongoing work of God recognise the fact that they serve a God 'who is able to do exceedingly abundantly above all that we ask or *think*'.[263] No matter our natural age, as 'partakers of the divine nature'[264] we inherently have the wherewithal to move beyond the narrow confines of society's ageist thinking. The godly

263. Ephesians 3:20, NASB, emphasis mine.
264. 2 Peter 1:4, NASB

nature of which born-again[265] believers partake is that of an 'extravagant' God, a loving heavenly Father who enjoys wandering outside the bounds of human expectation. To move beyond the margins of society's stereotypical view of age and the ageing process is perhaps the biggest challenge facing today's seniors!

There is said to be a roadside sign in Alaska that reads: 'Choose your rut carefully, you'll be in it for the next two hundred miles'. Over the passage of time, the traffic has created deep grooves in the one-time softened soil. Different people have over a period of time travelled in the same direction, doing exactly what their predecessors have done before. Their routine has created a rut, into which others travellers easily fall. When seniors revert to type, they fall into those rut-like patterns of behaviour which past generations have created over time.

To preserve the past in a way that hinders God's preferred future is unhelpful to the ongoing purpose of God in our lives. When seniors refuse to move with God-ordained change, they will not only feel the cold chill of isolation, but suffer the indignity of being dumped on society's scrapheap, whereas entrepreneur elders create new pathways, pioneering a different way of living life in the last lane.

However, rather than seeing themselves as entrepreneurial pathfinders, some retirees see themselves as decommissioned battleships beached on a far-flung eastern shore. Left high and dry, they await the indignity of death by dismantlement. Having had their day, they are systematically being stripped of their dignity and self-worth. Seen as spiritual relics

---

265. See John 3:1-8.

from a bygone era, they now lay idle, hidden and no longer deemed useful. Once seen as an essential part of a heavenly fighting force, they are fast becoming a mere shadow of their former self. Long gone are the days when they were engaged in battle. Viewed as an environmental embarrassment, these ageing vessels are being ignored, isolated and made to feel socially redundant. While some might reminisce about bygone battles, others ask why these ancient relics are being allowed to clutter the Christian landscape. Forcibly made to feel superfluous by monogenerational leaders who should know better, the elderly are experiencing an ignominious end to a lifetime in the service in God's kingdom.

Caleb culture

When experiencing an atmosphere of zero encouragement, third agers need to grab hold of divine hope and 'outrageously' run headlong through all opposing factors. Like the biblical character Caleb, they need to face each challenge with a godly attitude that enables them to fully enter into the promises of God over their lives. While others failed to view their surroundings through the eye of faith, Caleb maintained an alternative angle of approach, to which a loving heavenly Father commented, 'Because my servant Caleb has a different attitude . . . I will bring him into the land which he explored, and his descendants will possess the land'.[266]

---

266. Numbers 14:24, GNT.

Having transitioned the highs and lows of the wilderness years, Caleb maintained a mountaineering mindset well into his eighties. Cultivating a Caleb Culture is perhaps one of the greatest challenges facing third agers. Ploughing through the prejudicial hardened ground of present thinking, they need to develop a Christlike mindset.

Age is an attitude. For seniors to stand against the incoming tide of current thinking, they will need to respectfully contest for those mountains of inheritance that are rightfully theirs. To settle for the lowlands of isolation and invisibility is incomprehensible. By adopting a Caleb mindset, we are announcing to the world that our intentions are to ask organisational leaders to 'give [us the] hill country'.[267] Refusing to walk in the valleys of mediocrity, there's a geriatric generation of go-getters who reject the thought of retiring on some spiritual plateau. Snubbing the status quo that says sit back, take it easy, you've had your day, they push towards the zenith of all that God has promised. Etched into their final years will be the same epitaph spoken by Noel Odell, as he watched two pioneering greats push towards the summit of Everest. Speaking of his co-climbers, George Mallory and Andrew 'Sandy' Irvine and their tireless effort to be the first to successfully climb Mount Everest, Odell spoke of how they were last seen 'going strong for the top'.[268]

In an age when the ageing process is being challenged, we rejoice in the fact that some church leaders are learning how to recycle redundant retirees. Yet within this

---

267. Joshua 14:12, NASB.
268. www.merton.ox.ac.uk/library-and-archives/exhibitions/sandy-irvine-1924 (accessed 16.7.25).

challenging environment, third agers will need to adjust, and if necessary, alter their angle of approach to living life in the last lane. Growing old is not only different, it's difficult. It may be *true* that growing old is demanding, but the *truth* is that by God's grace we can all aspire to new levels of spiritual revelation and development as we climb the spiral staircase of life.

Other worldly

Increasingly out of touch with the world we live in, many seniors feel 'other worldly'. We might talk of ourselves as recycled teenagers, but the reality is, our minds are often cashing cheques that our bodies are unable to honour.

We come from a time when *windows* were a glazed opening in a wall. *Applications* were something written on a piece of paper. A *keyboard* was part of a piano and a *mouse,* something you set traps for. In our day a *file* was an important piece of information kept in a filing cabinet and a *hard drive* was an extended road trip. We grew up in a time when a *web* was created by a spider, a *virus* was flu and an *Apple* was just fruit. We are a rare and dying breed who speak a different language, think and value different things.

But if anyone expects us to sit quietly in the corner while everyone else chatters on – think again. As long as there is breath in our ageing bodies, we are determined to live our remaining years thinking and doing the unexpected. Refusing to 'go gently into that long good night,'[269] we intend our final notes to formulate a glorious crescendo.

---

269. Dylan Thomas (1914-53), 'Do Not Go Gentle into that Good Night', published 1951.

Knowing the sands of time are fast running out, our faith is in a loving heavenly Father who might grant us sufficient time to do one more godly exploit. As supersonic saints, we intend to live each day with a heartfelt passion that says, 'If we're not dead, then God's not done!' So being told to act our age in a disparaging way is not God's view of ageing, it's ageism. Rather than allowing our lives to lay fallow, God fully expects our senior years to be fruitful. The psalmist puts it this way: 'They still bear fruit in old age; they are ever full of sap and green, to declare that the LORD is upright; he is my rock'. [270]

Life with limits

Living life in the last lane comes with physical, financial and social limitations. Such confinements can be either viewed as restrictive or releasing. With clearly defined boundaries, the apostle Paul spoke in terms of a 'sphere of influence'.[271] Just as an Olympic javelin competitor would have their throwing distance measured to determine the extent of their reach, the apostle acknowledged a measured geographical 'sphere of service'[272] and the people within which he was determined to reach with the good news about the risen, glorified Christ.

No matter the age or stage of life we find ourselves, we all have specific spheres of influence, a given area in which to serve the purpose of God. Whether it's our neighbourhood, social group, hospital, coffee shop or people entering

270. Psalm 92:14-15, ESV.
271. See 2 Corinthians 10:13-14.
272. 2 Corinthians 10:13, TNIV.

our home, there is still a range of people that we can influence. This 'sphere of service' is a measured mission field. Although we may no longer travel the world, by God's grace the world is coming to us. No matter how seemingly restrictive our circumstances, there is always a possibility to involve ourselves in the affairs of heaven on earth.

The Hebrides Revival (1949-52) was a significant spiritual awakening in the Scottish Islands. However, the spark that ignited this flame was the fervent prayers of two elderly sisters, Peggy and Christine Smith. Burdened by the spiritual decline in their village church, the sisters, in their eighties and unable to attend regular services due to Peggy's blindness and Christine's arthritis, committed themselves to weekly prayer. Their consistent and persistent intercessory prayer for a fresh move of God – along with the ministry of Duncan Campbell – led to a widespread spiritual awakening. Accepting life's limitations, they gave themselves to pray for that specific sphere of influence in which they found themselves. Refusing to be hampered by the physical limitations, they reached out in faith to bring heaven to earth.

No matter how limited life might become, by God's grace we can engage in the affairs of heaven on earth. If the biblical Joseph served the purposes of God in servitude, Daniel while surrounded by wild animals, the apostle Paul from prison, the prophet Elijah alone in the wilderness and John exiled on an island, surely we can with God's grace bring heaven to earth no matter our circumstance or surroundings?

We don't stop living because we grow old;
we grow old because we stop living.

Question marks!

- Do you tend to see life's limitations as an obstacle to overcome or an opportunity to share God's good news?

- Take a moment to list possible spheres of influence you are presently involved in:

  Sphere 1

  Sphere 2

  Sphere 3

Now ask God to give you the wherewithal to bring the Christian message into these various spheres of influence.

Printed in Dunstable, United Kingdom

68124425R00137